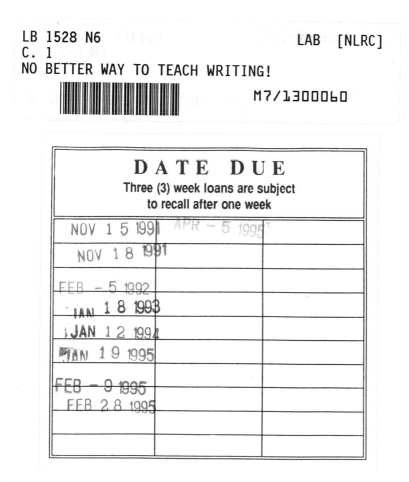

No better way to teach writing!

edited by JAN TURBILL
Language Consultant,
St. George Region, N.S.W. Department of Education

ADVISORY PANEL

Barbara Fiala
Infants Mistress, Sylvania Heights Primary School

Robyn Legge
Infants Mistress, Hurstville South Primary School

Robyn Platt
Infants Mistress, Grays Point Primary School

R. D. Walshe
Publications Editor, P.E.T.A.

Distributed in the U.S.A.
by
HEINEMANN EDUCATIONAL BOOKS, INC.
70 Court Street
Portsmouth, New Hampshire 03801

PETA

PRIMARY ENGLISH TEACHING ASSOCIATION

Acknowledgments

When the Primary English Teaching Association invited me to 'put a book together on the teachers' impressions of the St. George Writing Project', my first thought was, 'Why not?' We were always *talking* about it, so why not share our thoughts with other teachers in *writing*? The idea quickly took hold of my imagination. I was thrilled that P.E.T.A. President Barry Dwyer and the Council had realised the great potential of this new approach and wanted to rush our news of it to teachers all over Australia.

But surely the suggestion had come too late — October of the project year! I didn't know much about 'putting a book together'. My heart sank when Publications Editor Bob Walshe said, 'You'll have to ask the teachers to write their accounts in November then do your editing in December so that we can do our editing in January, print in February and mail out in March, in time for teachers to use the ideas in programming — otherwise you'll lose a year!' Impossible! But with his ever-present guiding and writing hand and hard work, we have somehow managed to keep the appointment.

The St. George Writing Project didn't just happen. It involved many people and needed careful organisation throughout the year. For unwavering support and encouragement I want to thank the Principals and Infants Mistresses of the three project schools, Mr. Trevor Harrison, St. George Regional Director, and Mr. Eric Flood, Inspector of Studies/Services and Chairman of the Regional English Language Committee K-12.

All 27 of the project teachers wrote reports for the book. It is their year-long work and last-minute writing that give the book what I believe is its special flavour — a blend of their aroused interest, their pleasure in the children's progress, and their excitement in making discoveries and exhanging them. I also want to thank the other teachers who have contributed, especially the groups in South Australia, Victoria and the Liverpool Region of N.S.W. Their independent testimonies to the power and effectiveness of the 'conference approach' have of course delighted us.

Many other teachers and friends have helped either the project or the production of the book. Barbara Kamler and Gary Kilarr of Riverina C.A.E. provided an in-service day early in the year and another at mid-year, making available their extensive knowledge of the research work of Donald H. Graves and his associates of the University of New Hampshire. Barry Caesar, teacher at Gymea Bay Public School, spent a morning in each of the project schools taking most of the book's photos during writing sessions. Terry Jeff took the cover photo. Jan Gilmore-Smith, Tony Moore, and Trevor Cairney contributed insights from their own trialling of the approach. Val Fryer, Emily Lawrence and Judith Walker handled the rush of typing. And, as usual, John Rough met P.E.T.A.'s 'latest, completely unreasonable printing deadline'.

I have purposely left till last my thanks to the children. The teachers and I have experienced many exciting moments watching them write and talking to them about their writing. Their enthusiasm and their desire to write have inspired us. What's more, they have made me want to write too! —J.T.

Cover design by Dorothy Dunphy

Cover photo: Marilyn Rigg, Sylvania Heights Primary School, in conference with a Year 1 child, while writing partners discuss their work. In the left background are some of her children's 'published' stories.

ISBN 0 909955 39 5

First published March 1982
Reprinted August 1982
Reprinted April 1983
Reprinted August 1984
© **Primary English Teaching Association**
P.O. Box 167, Rozelle, N.S.W. 2039 (02) 818 2591
Printed in Australia by
Bridge Printery Pty Ltd, 29-35 Dunning Ave, Rosebery, N.S.W. 2018

Contents

Part 1: The Conference Approach K-2

Part 2: In the Primary School

'Yes, Children Do Want to Write . . .'

FOREWORD

by Eric Flood
Inspector of Studies/Services
St. George Region
N.S.W. Department of Education

'Children want to write. For years we have underestimated their urge to make marks on a page . . .' The address that followed these opening words excited me. The speaker was Professor Donald H. Graves and I was attending the Third International English Teaching Conference, held at Sydney University in August 1980.

Until that evening I had known little of Graves or the painstaking classroom research undertaken by his Writing Process Laboratory in New Hampshire, U.S.A. But as I joined in the enthusiastic applause at the end I felt sure I would be hearing a great deal more about the man and his sane approach to children's writing.

How right that prediction has proved! Discussion of his ideas has continued Australia-wide. But I could not have predicted that the approach would be trialled more comprehensively in a selected group of schools of the St. George Region than anywhere else in Australia. Credit for this must largely go to the initiative and year-long application of Jan Turbill, a Language Consultant in the Region, together with the Infants Mistresses of the three project schools and their 27 teachers.

The important story assembled here by these teachers needs no comment from me. I do, however, want to point to a noteworthy corollary: the project demonstrates the great potential of 'classroom action research'. For here are 27 teachers, fairly arbitrarily chosen from thousands of others, who have convincingly risen to the onerous challenge of researching and reporting on how-to-teach-writing, a teaching problem as complex as any we face.

It must be stated that the Writing Project was planned with care. Key regional personnel were consulted, maintained contact and were kept informed of developments. At all times, the process has been an example of change brought about by dedicated teachers within a framework of no less dedicated management.

This proves that similar 'action research' can be planned, initiated and managed by groups of teachers anywhere — everywhere! If they do so, I hope they will be as fortunate as our project teachers in having P.E.T.A. offer its services for the designing, publishing and distributing of an attractive book — all within three months of the conclusion of the Project's first year.

About This New Approach

'What's so different *and new* about this approach to writing?'

Chiefly that, instead of tight teacher-control of the what, when and how of writing, the child is given control of the writing ('ownership' or 'responsibility'). This is a significant shift of focus, from teaching to learning, and it changes the writing program in important ways:

- the program is completely individualised
- the child makes responsible decisions about what to write
- there is daily time to 'learn to write by writing' (*quantity*)
- the child can discover his or her unique way or 'process' of writing
- there is time to talk individually with the teacher — 'in conference'
- the conference attends to making the writing better (*quality*).

This book describes a year's 'action research' by 27 teachers, the St. George Project, a comprehensive trial of the 'process-conference approach to the teaching of writing' — or 'conference approach' as it was soon dubbed — an approach that respects the child's control of the 'process-of-writing' (topic-choice, pre-writing, drafting, revising, publishing) and moves forward through teacher-child 'conferencing'.

In making this report on the teachers' views of the Project, I have faced an editorial choice: whether to synthesise their statements in a generalised pronouncement or to preserve as much as possible of their individuality and insight? To follow the second course would involve, I knew, some overlapping but I have unhesitatingly chosen to do this because it shows the teachers, through their own words, 'learning by doing'.

Neither they nor I wish to convey that here is THE CORRECT WAY; rather, here is the best we have managed so far. There is of course more to learn, and we are looking forward to next year's opportunity to pursue the approach further.

What I have found inspiring is the speed with which all the teachers have developed in their understanding of 'children writing', after the teething problems of the first weeks. On the other hand, we know that, as in all teaching, when one problem is solved a new, higher-level problem presents itself. Still, the end of the year left all of us with the entirely positive feeling that *we are as much in control of our teaching as the children are of their writing*.

The concentration of the Project is on the early — the basic! — years of writing. This is deliberate and necessary. All subsequent trial or implementation of the approach can now build on a solid foundation. After all, the child who has discovered in these early years an individual writing *process*, as these children have done, is only going to develop *in degree* thereafter, whether in primary or secondary school, gradually lifting quantity, content, style, and control of a variety of modes year by year. This is why every teacher has an obligation to know what happens in the K-2 years, those years when the unspoiled child learns to write. The lessons for later years are immense!

We share our work openly and honestly with readers in the conviction that there is no better way to teach writing — *and*, at the same time, reading . . . Nor any better way to raise children's confidence as learners.

Part I: The Conference Approach K-2

CHAPTER 1

Launching the Conference Approach

At surprising speed the 'conference approach' to the teaching of writing is gripping the imagination of Australian teachers. No one can say exactly how many of them are trying out the approach in their classrooms, but their numbers are obviously growing quickly.

This book is centrally a report of a year's trialling of the approach by 27 teachers in three Sydney primary schools—the 'St. George Writing Project K-2'[1]—but so many other teachers have sent me illuminating accounts of similar, smaller projects that I am able to add an instructive sampling of them, chiefly for Years 3-6.

How the St. George Project Started

Our story begins with the visit of Donald Graves to Australia in August 1980.

The Primary English Teaching Association (P.E.T.A.), aware of his innovative research into the teaching of writing, had specially invited Professor Donald H. Graves to Sydney for the Third International Conference

Donald Graves

on the Teaching of English. His impact on the Conference has been reported in a P.E.T.A. book, *Donald Graves in Australia* (ed. R. D. Walshe, 120 pp.),[2] which, as well as so far selling 14 thousand copies in this country, has sold a further thousand in the United States.

I was fortunate. Not only did I hear Graves' Conference address but I talked in some detail with him afterwards. His message excited me but I was unsure what to do about it.

When I later visited Sylvania Heights Primary School the Infants Mistress, Barbara Fiala, told me that she too had felt excited and wanted

---

[1] The schools of the New South Wales Department of Education are divided among eleven educational regions, one of which is St. George, on the south side of Sydney, with 100 primary and 30 secondary schools.

[2] The book contains also his address to the Conference and ten authoritative articles by researchers and teachers associated with the Writing Process Laboratory of the University of New Hampshire.

to do something. We had both reached the same conclusion: 'Why haven't the schools been teaching writing in this commonsense way all along?' Barbara then invited me to work on the 'conference approach' with an interested teacher on her staff, Marie Mann. In fact, 'Why not start at once?'

We Attempt a Trial Run

We were then in last term. Don Graves had warned me against brief research episodes — development in writing takes time! However, I badly needed to get the feel of the new approach and Marie was eager. She asked many questions and I left three articles for her to read . . . So, on a bright September morning, little more than a month after Graves left Australia, Marie and I introduced her Year 1 children to 'a new and better way to go about our writing and drawing'.

My worry was that I could only visit the school irregularly. Marie cheerfully suggested that while she worked with the rest of the class I should spend whatever time I had working with four 'case studies', four children carefully selected to represent the class's ability· range. In this team-teaching situation I began to interview my quartet, collect pieces of their writing, and diarise their feelings towards writing.

Lessons of the Trial

Late in November we compared the writing of our 'experimental group' with that of a 'control group' of four children also carefully selected to represent the ability range of the parallel Year I class next door. We collected work written in August (pre-trial), September, October, November — 32 pieces in all. (Each piece had been prepared for publication, so that spelling and punctuation had been edited for correctness.)

Two English Language Consultants rated this writing as *very good* (A), *good* (B), *average* (C), or *poor* (D). Their criteria were kept to three considerations: quality of sentence structure, orderliness of thought, clarity of expression. Here are the results:

Table 1: Experimental Group

	Aug.	Sept.	Oct.	Nov.
Susan	C	A	A	A
Karen	C	A	A	A
Fred	C	B	B	A
Sean	D	A	B	B

Table 2: Control Group

	Aug.	Sept.	Oct.	Nov.
Ashley	C	D	C	B
Christa	C	C	C	C
David	D	C	B	C
Maria	D	D	D	D

We were delighted. Notable were the very positive scores of the experimental group, their astonishingly rapid improvement (in the first month) which was a tribute to the spirit engendered by the approach, and the sureness with which they sustained and built upon their early gains. We know that our little experiment was less than rigorous, yet we have no hesitation in inviting others to replicate this 'action research', which, in its simplicity, is within the scope of busy classroom teachers.

Even more importantly, the children had enjoyed their writing and they regularly looked forward to it. Marie and I agreed that we had learnt a

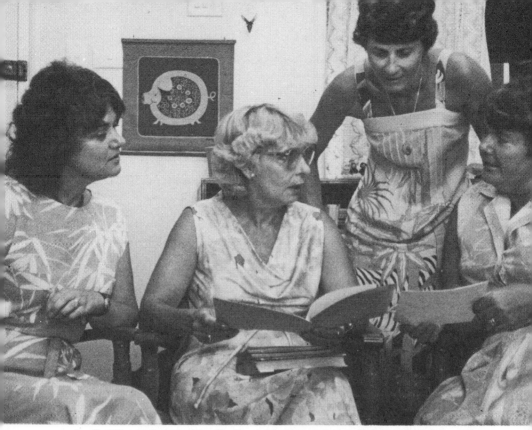

Jan Turbill, coordinator of the St. George Project, met regularly with the Mistresses from the three schools, Robyn Legge, Barbara Fiala and Robyn Platt.

great deal about the writing process in general and young children's writing development in particular. In these two areas our rate of learning was as rapid as the children's in theirs. We realised — often guiltily! — that our previous approaches to teaching writing had largely thwarted the children's efforts. Above all, *we had greatly underestimated their potential desire to write and potential ability to handle written expression.*

We were slower in appreciating what we took to be only a side benefit: the children were eager to *read* one another's writing. The 'books' they wrote became the most frequently used segment of the class library. At last Marie observed, 'You know, their reading has improved as much as their writing'. We were thrilled.

Marie also felt certain that their spelling and punctuation skills had considerably improved. They were using more punctuation marks than the 'normal' Year 1 child. However, she reserved her main praise for the change in classroom spirit:

'The whole class get on far better than before. They help each other. They are far more reliable and self-confident, and I find I never have to yell. It may be that I know them better because of the many conferences we've had; while they, in turn, know that I know them. Whatever it is, I've never had a better term. It's rewarding to realise that not only am I enjoying teaching writing but also that the children enjoy learning to write. Now other teachers at Sylvania Heights are asking me how they should start.'

Launching the Larger Project

The trial run had helped me in many ways but I knew I had a great deal more to learn, especially through observing the children and listening to them tell me how I could help them.

The St. George Regional English Language Committee K-12 agreed that I should widen the work in 1981. All the teachers in the Infants Departments of three schools were willing to take part: Grays Point (6 teachers), Hurstville South (9 teachers), and Sylvania Heights (12 teachers). The project would run for a year and then be evaluated.

Mr Eric Flood, the chairman of the Regional In-service Program, strongly supported the project and prevailed on me to write a proposal which could be given to the teachers. 'It's a writing project,' he said emphatically, 'so the least you can do is put some writing into your teachers' hands instead of relying on a talk.' I grumbled at the work this would mean for me, but I knew he was right. Here, in a slightly amended form, is what resulted . . .

Proposal

A proposal to the teachers who have agreed to take part in the St. George Writing Project K-2

Dear Colleague

Thank you for agreeing to join this year-long experiment in teaching writing by the 'process-conference approach'.

The purpose of this proposal is to outline the approach, using ideas that come chiefly from its principal researcher Donald H. Graves of the University of New Hampshire's Writing Process Laboratory and from our own trialling of the approach at Sylvania Heights Primary School.

1. Philosophy Underlying the Project

After years of relative neglect, writing is rapidly acquiring equal status with reading. Justly so, for reading and writing are the two sides of the coin of literacy. Given a chance, they interweave and reinforce each other. So much so that some teachers are now saying, 'The best way to teach reading is to get children writing', and others that 'A love of reading is the best way to foster a love of writing'.

Learning to write is usually seen as a difficult process, e.g.,

> 'Writing is a complex task, often entailing a long and slow development. The process of writing involves many thinking skills: generating ideas, organising ideas and expressing ideas. Writing will be most rewarding when the child is encouraged to write without the inhibition of an overemphasis on formal skills, and when his or her work is willingly accepted by the teacher and fellow pupils.' (*N.S.W. Primary Lang. Curriculum, 1974*)

But Donald Graves never stresses the difficulties. He strongly believes

> 'that children want to write. For years we have underestimated
> their urge to make marks on paper. We have underestimated
> that urge because of a lack of understanding of the writing
> process, and what children do in order to control it. Without
> realising it, we wrest control away from the children and place
> road blocks that thwart their intentions. Then we say, "They
> don't want to write. What is a good way to motivate them?" . . .
> If children are to be in control of their writing we need to give
> them more opportunity to write, allow them to write about what
> they know, allow them to choose the materials they want to write
> with (pencil, crayon, large paper, lined paper etc.), and allow
> them the opportunity to write for themselves initially (a draft
> copy).'[3]

His research has established that children can write at 5-6 years old,
that they enjoy doing it, and that at this age they can make the most
rapid and delightful growth in writing of their entire lives. He argues
that every child at all ages needs to be given regular opportunities to
discover and develop his or her unique writing process and to apply
this process to a wide range of writing tasks.

He stresses that other forms of expression, drawing, drama and
talking, play a vital role in the writing process by allowing children to
sort out their thoughts and ideas, and thus work out what they want
to express. For example, drawing may precede the writing as part of
the prewriting stage. It can also have a useful function when the
writing is finished, filling in details not mentioned in the story and
thus completing the process for the child.

Talking is important at both the prewriting and drafting stages.
The children need to talk a great deal both audibly and sub-audibly,
as if directing themselves as to what they should write next. They
re-read and sound out words. They ask questions of each other for
information and generally discuss their work in order to clarify
meaning. Talk is thus an aid in the hard work of composing, but
eventually it becomes internalised as the 'inner speech' used by adults
in the writing process.

Graves also stresses that children need to be able to write freely
without interruption to their thought. He draws attention to the
value of 'invented spelling' for allowing learners to use vocabulary
from their oral language and so flow on in their writing instead of
avoiding words whose spelling is not known. Too much correction at
the wrong time, he argues, can be dangerous. In fact, concentration
on error, instead of leading to correct spelling, can reinforce a child's
self-doubt.

Graves places very strong emphasis on the importance of the 'conference'. This usually takes the form of a one-to-one conversation
between the teacher and child about the purpose, content and style
of the child's writing. Graves has found that all the mechanics and all

---

[3] *Donald Graves in Australia*, ed. R. D. Walshe (P.E.T.A., 1981), p. 17 *ff*.

the grammar children need to know in the primary school can be adequately taught in the conference, instead of through generalised whole-class exercises. He argues:

> 'Writing is a marvellous unifier . . . We teachers have yet to make proper use of its power in securing the deepest kinds of learning, in improving children's critical thinking, and in integrating the curriculum.

> 'Consider any whole piece of original writing done by any child in the junior school: here is the handwriting, spelling, punctuation, grammar and usage that skills-teaching is supposed to be about. But looked at intelligently this piece leaves little need for separate skills teaching. The teacher has only to examine the piece to see what this child needs. Specific help can then be given. This is teaching in context, at the point of need.'[4]

Writing is important; it is important in every year of school learning and in careers and social life beyond school. Fully realising this, the process-conference approach urges the necessity of providing time for writing *every day*. The case for doing so is unanswerable.

2. What It Means for Our Classrooms

For implementing these ideas, the following classroom procedures are suggested:

1. The children will be given the time and responsibility to write every day, for half an hour. They can write a new story each day or continue working on yesterday's writing. If they are not happy about a piece, they can start it again, or write something different. The decision is theirs.
2. The teacher no longer assigns writing tasks. The children will choose their own topics and keep control of their writing at all stages.
3. The children's control (or 'ownership') of their writing will also be fostered by
   - using a Writing Folder for storing all pieces of writing;
   - making sheets of paper available, unlined and lined, in a variety of sizes, colours, and sometimes shapes (but some children prefer to write in a book);
   - considering first writing to be a 'draft' which can usually be improved by additions, cuts, crossings-out, rearrangements and other 'self-editing' measures;
   - encouraging 'invented spelling' as an important aid in learning to spell;
   - not over-emphasising handwriting neatness;
   - allowing freedom of movement within the room, such as choosing where to sit, visiting other children to show work or converse (within reason), and making use of the classroom library.

---

[4] *Ibid.*, p. 15.

4. Drawing will be considered integral to the writing process at this stage, with children given the option to draw before, during or after the writing, and encouraged to discuss their drawings.
5. 'Publication' will be promoted. The children will choose from the drafts in their Folders a favoured one and discuss with the teacher the reasons for their choice. By no means all drafts will be published (perhaps one in four); but all drafts will be dated and kept as a record of progress. Publication involves
   - setting down the 'story' so that the reader can follow the author's intended meaning;
   - attractive presentation through neat handwriting, correct spelling, helpful punctuation, good page lay-out (or by typing, using school or parent help);
   - illustration, whether by drawing or painting, and also stylish headings;
   - presentation to interested readers — immediately to the teacher and classmates, and later perhaps to other classes and parents;
   - preparation of the 'book' for a long life — by binding in durable covers, with title, author's name, cover design, date of publication and whatever other attributes are noticed by the children in commercially produced books;
   - placing of the 'book' in the class or school library.
6. The 'conference' will be seen as the centrepoint of classroom interaction and a great teaching art to be mastered. Several conferences may be needed before a piece of writing is ready for publication. In conference the teacher
   - talks with the child or group of children about topic-choice, ways to begin, where the story is going, etc.;
   - helps the child with the continuity of the story, so that it reads as the child wants it;
   - tries to identify conventions of writing the child may need (punctuation, spelling, grammar), only one or two of these becoming a teaching point in any one conference and then chiefly at the 'polishing' stage and in preparation for publication;
   - listens or reads as the child's first audience — a role which the children gradually emulate, so that their 'peer conferencing' increasingly eases the pressure on the teacher.

Early Responses to the Proposal

From the first days, the teachers experienced successes with the new approach while the children, with a few temporary exceptions, happily adapted to it. Of course there were early difficulties, doubts, questions.

Thinking back to the teachers' early responses, I offer the following advice to readers who wish to try the approach:
- An in-service program on the approach can certainly help, but it is not essential — many teachers have started successfully after only reading about it.

- Read as much as you can from three sources available from P.E.T.A.: (1) this book, (2) *Donald Graves in Australia*, ed. R. D. Walshe, (3) the same author's *Every Child Can Write!*, which contains a 20-page summary of the approach together with over 200 more pages of ideas about writing.[5]
- Work together as a grade or whole staff, supporting one another and meeting problems as they arise. (If you wish to make an individual start, try first to win the support of your executive staff.) Seek the help of your Language Consultant or of teachers in other schools who have experienced the approach.
- Don't expect too much too soon. When children who are habituated to being told what to write and how to write it are given control of their writing, it may seem initially to regress in quality and quantity. But, given time, this will change.
- Especially the free choice of topics may at first bewilder some children—till patient conferencing wins them to valuing this important freedom.
- Be prepared to change direction a little if things aren't going well: your class and you are embarked on a considerable change in learning style. Feel your way flexibly.
- Communicate regularly with parents. Don't be surprised if they mistrust a departure from traditional methods. Not only explain what you are doing but invite them to help (in ways that are indicated later). They can become powerful allies in the work.

Phases in the St. George Project

The following notes sketch some phases in our project. They may provide ideas useful to some readers, but others may develop a project rather differently.

- *Reporting.* Throughout the year I consulted and reported to the Regional Director, Trevor Harrison, the Studies/Services Inspector, Eric Flood, and Inspectors concerned with the three schools.
- *Planning.* At about monthly intervals I met the Executive Staff of each school to plan aspects of the approach. Their support was vital.
- *Staff Meetings.* An initial staff meeting in each school discussed the project (after studying the proposal). Teachers of each grade came together from the three schools at after-school meetings, held monthly, to discuss problems and share samples of writing. The opportunity to exchange experiences across schools was rewarding. Usually the meetings took an hour and a half.
- *Consultancy.* I spent half a day each week in each school during the first term, discussing classroom organisation and teaching strategies. Often I worked with the children to experience the problems and pleasures of their teachers. I supplemented the monthly grade meetings by transmitting ideas from school to school and generally tried to monitor the project. By the third term I felt that the teachers needed very little support.

---

[5] A fourth and very important source is promised by the publisher for late 1982: *Writing: Teachers and Children at Work*, by Donald H. Graves (Heinemann Educational).

They had become 'inservicers' to a swelling stream of educators who came to their schools to observe at first hand.

- *In-Service Training.* Two in-service days were organised for the teachers.[6] The first, in March, was an introduction to the process-conference approach and it included practical experience of 'process' (rehearsing/drafting/revising/publishing) together with 'control of one's own writing'. The second, in June, concentrated on the issues the teachers wished to discuss at that stage of the project.

- *Evaluation.* This was very much an ongoing process, which continually prompted the teachers to modify their practices to meet emerging needs. So individual is 'conferencing' that a teacher becomes sharply aware of every child's strengths and weaknesses. The teachers shared their impressions at the monthly grade meetings which were opportunities for self-evaluation and evaluation of the project in general.

- *New Questions Arise.* Some questions from the teachers can only be answered with more time than the single year of our project. For instance:
  - .. What will happen when these Year 2 children move to a new teacher in Year 3?
  - .. What will the Kindergarten children be able to do from the beginning of Year 1?
  - .. How should I be 'teaching reading' now that I know this writing approach strongly assists reading?
  - .. Can I fully integrate writing, reading, spelling and other aspects of language?
  - .. How does this approach assist the acquisition of English by E.S.L. learners?

Why This Book?

Without setting down our story in book form we can't cope with the requests for information that are coming in from many parts of Australia and New Zealand. Moreover, in the latter part of the year over 200 classroom teachers, tertiary teachers and student teachers visited the schools and they invariably asked for 'A written summing-up of the Project — when you get round to it!'

So by dint of a vacation given over to writing and massively helped, first, by a written statement from all of the participating teachers, second, by the Advisory Panel, and third, by a crash printing production by P.E.T.A. — helped by all these, we hope to have this book in the hands of teachers all over Australia by March, in time to make 1982 a year of wide diffusion of this 'Better Way to Teach Writing' (and, we firmly believe, Reading too!).

---

[6] Both in-service days were led by Barbara Kamler and Gary Kilarr, lecturers at Riverina College of Advanced Education. Barbara had spent six months working with Donald Graves.

CHAPTER 2

Getting Started

As we embarked on our new program we felt both excitement and mis-giving. Why change from the 'old order' by which most of our children had seemed to learn to write? . . . Well, perhaps we might become better teachers of writing, might really enjoy teaching writing, might even over-come the reluctance that so many children develop towards writing.

'On Your Marks, Get Set . . .'
The teachers, I believe, felt moderately well prepared; they
.. had studied the *Proposal* outlining the project (see p. 10);
.. had been given access to wider reading;
.. had talked together as a staff, and with the Consultant;
.. knew they could refer problems to their Infants Mistress;
.. knew they should keep their parents informed;
.. had been advised not to expect too much in the first weeks;
.. were ready with a trial form of classroom organisation; and
.. had considered the resources needed in their rooms (see p. 24).

Final Briefings
My anxiety kept me inflicting advice on any of the teachers who crossed my path in the early weeks. I must have strained their tolerance. Mostly I made points like:

- 'It's a big change. We're giving the children *control* of their own writing and learning — an opportunity to *discover* their own writing pro-cess. Will we really be able to trust these little ones as much as that? Will we be able to leave the pencil in the child's hand? Or will we uncon-sciously fall into the old directive, do-as-I-tell-you ways?'

- 'Don't expect too much *at first*. The children won't instantly switch from teacher-control to self-control of their writing. We've been warned that, with their attention fixed on new responsibilites, many will seem to slip backward from skills they've used before — but given time they will soon pick up any lost ground and move ahead strongly.'

Getting My Kindergarten Started: Pat Robertson[1]
Though feeling insecure about this new approach, I placed paper, pencils and crayons on the tables and said to my four and five year olds, 'Write anything you can — write as much as you can.' To my surprise only a few said they didn't know how, but even they were quite happy when asked to 'Just have a try'.

---

[1] Pat Robertson's 28 kindergarten children come from many ethnic backgrounds, including several non-English speaking ones.

The results of that first day's efforts ranged through:
.. wriggly lines
.. something like hieroglyphics
.. lists of letters and numerals
.. the children's names and those of siblings
.. lists of unconnected words, e.g. *stop   Shell   BP*
.. a page of a Lebanese girl's version of Arabic writing
.. combinations of words and pictures, e.g. *My* [cat drawn] *got 2* [kittens drawn], sometimes with an oral explanation, e.g. 'I don't know how to write some words, so I draw the pictures'.
.. one child wrote *NKT . Sunday . IS . esdea . Sunday* and explained that the dots tell when to start a new word.

My first big problem immediately became evident: all the children wanted to talk to me about their writing—*NOW!* I was being run off my feet. I began consulting other teachers and eventually decided to try working intensively with only one group each day. This meant constantly reminding children that I could only cope with 'today's group'. I encouraged the rest to talk to one another and share their writing and drawing.

By degrees the class adjusted to the new way of working. We now begin our writing time by reading the latest 'published' books and then we move to our writing groups. This organisation didn't achieve perfection. Some children coped well, others made the best of it (knowing I was available to help if big difficulties arose), but there remained a number who weren't

Pat Robertson has noted that her Kindergarten's discoveries in writing have sharpened their powers of observation and their interest in reading.

ready to write day after day unless I was right there with them. These lagging ones were wasting time but I judged that they really did want to write. So I changed my timetable to allow for writing with them at a later time when the rest of the class were involved in other activities. This is proving quite successful.

My other major problem took a few weeks to surface. Some of the more able children became dissatisfied with what they were producing. They wanted to 'get it right'. They were disinclined to write words they were not sure of spelling, though I assured them that only an attempt was required of them. I was worried that they would stop writing their own thoughts and so compel me to go back to supplying them with *my* words. In retrospect I think this was no more than a brief developmental stage for some children — it seemed to be connected with their beginning to read and it passed as they became involved in a 'mix' of reading, language and writing activities. At first the fact that they were writing sharpened their observation of what they were reading and accelerated their development of reading skills; later the reading seemed to give confidence to those who became disinclined to write, so that they started writing again.

Despite these and lesser problems, I am very impressed by the writing my (now) five and six year olds are producing. Of course not all the writing is instantly readable by adult standards but the general progress is really surprising. Nearly every child has come must further than I would have thought possible only eight months ago.

Getting My Year 1 Started: Debbie Brownjohn

I found I needed several discussions with the children before we started on this new approach. I explained that we would be writing every day for half an hour on topics of their choosing and could use any writing implements and paper available.

● *'Invented Spelling'*. By 'inventing' their spelling instead of waiting for spellings from me they would get their thoughts onto paper quickly — 'inventing' meant writing as many sounds as they could hear in a word or writing the part of the word they could hear or see in their minds.

● *Drawing*. I explained that drawing a picture was also a way of telling a story. Drawing was very important to most of them in the beginning, a starting point for their stories; but as their writing developed, it became less important. (At the end of the year, I find that they want to illustrate their 'published' books — but I consider this a different function for drawing, an addition to the writing.)

● *Sheets or Books?* At first the children worked on single sheets of paper. With usually only one sentence on a sheet they had difficulty continuing the story for several days, especially when their Writing Folders became cluttered and they couldn't easily find yesterday's sheet. I began stapling a number of sheets together for those who wanted them. We termed these our 'Empty Books'. They produced interest in composing sequential stories (at first with one sentence on each page) written over several days. At the end of each week I began collecting and storing all their finished drafts, whether in the form of the stapled books or loose sheets.

Children in Debbie Brownjohn's Year 1 invite constructive questioning after having shared their draft pieces with the class.

● *Parent Aides.* One of my greatest problems was the 'conference', the time to talk with the children individually. While I was talking with one, the 29 others might be needing my attention. I felt torn into 30 pieces. Fortunately some parents had volunteered to help. They were quickly accepted by the children, whether in the role of listening and responding to stories or helping out with stapling, supply of paper or other mechanical tasks. Their help was invaluable—even one parent in the room made a great difference.

● *Peer-editing.* As the children developed, they became less reliant on adults and more reliant on their peers. They really enjoy helping one another! They read one another's stories, comment on them, ask questions, show that a word or punctuation has been omitted, and point to parts that don't make sense. They learn a great deal by talking in this way and allow me more time to conference with individuals.

● *Publication.* This was at first a big problem. They wanted to publish everything they wrote! Together we made a class rule: 'Choose one story, the one *you* think is best, from the three or four you have written recently'. They also decided that it had to be read to at least two children for editing and proofreading. Then this 'best story' would go in the 'Publications Box'; the author would write his or her name on the list, which was never long, and await a conference with me. While waiting the child could begin

Christa Hunt reports: 'The thing that saved my sanity and enthusiasm was my decision to work with just one group each day.'

another story, help someone else, illustrate previously published stories, or read some of the many class-written or bought books in the class library.

The year hasn't been easy. Often I felt unsure of what I was doing, at times even frustrated and depressed. But it was all worth it. I feel happy now with the way the class is working. They seem to be in full control of what they are doing. I never thought that 6 and 7 year olds could write such fantastic stories.

Be Prepared to Change Course: Christa Hunt (Year 1)

At first I didn't appear to be getting anywhere. Conference time was too limited, the queue of children waiting on me grew longer, their sentences seemed stilted and not personal, 'invented spelling' wasn't working, the noise level was high . . . I felt like giving up.

But after discussion with my colleagues I decided to try some new measures:

- write an 'invented spelling' story on the board so all could see how it is done;
- read aloud some of the children's stories and show their efforts at invented spelling;
- occasionally spend a lesson brainstorming exciting topics and listing them for anyone's free choice;

- introduce an Ideas Box — plastic covered pictures and cards brought in by the children;
- examine the format and topics of commercial books, noting that they take longer to write than our one day per story;
- staple four sheets of paper together to make a book (offering such books in different sizes);
- keep my own folder-file for each child's stories, dating each piece for reference (each child would never have more than four current pieces of writing under the desk);
- encourage sharing of rough drafts, so discussion might produce improvement of spelling and punctuation;
- add incentive by 'publishing' — that is, typing completed stories and binding them as small books;
- organise 'writing partners', mainly to stimulate story ideas, but also to help with inventing spelling (also to find words, e.g. by ransacking library books for dinosaur words and spellings), and to satisfy the need for someone to talk and read to;
- give constant positive encouragement to the children, first about the content, second the mechanics, of their stories.

All these measures helped to bring the improvement I hoped for, but I have left till last the measure I consider most beneficial in saving my sanity: *I resolved to work with only one group each day.* This enabled me to become less teacher-centred and more child-centred because

- I was constantly thrilled at seeing what the children could do;
- I could work closely with every child at least once a week and knew what he or she was doing;
- without having to think when I saw each child last, I knew how much each was doing;
- I was with one group but also in the midst of others, and the general noise level dropped;
- I was close to the children's 'point of need', could observe their difficulties, respond to their questions, and discover how they developed their original thought by talking and trying out ideas.

I know my children better and they know I'm interested in them. I feel more confident not only in teaching writing but in teaching generally. The children too have grown more sensitive to one another's needs. Our classroom has become a happy place to work.

Getting Started in Term 3: Therese Corben (Year 2)

As a casual teacher I found myself thrust into a conference-approach classroom in Term 3. In my case it was the teacher, not the children, who had to 'get started'. The children had to *teach me* what they had been doing in the two previous terms.

I was apprehensive because teaching writing had always seemed a chore: I'd had problems with choosing topics, motivating them, and knowing what to do with the child who finishes in ten minutes what takes others half an hour — my writing classroom could become chaotic!

To my surprise I found that this class of 'remedial' Seconds really loved 'story writing time'. They looked forward to every day's writing. In fact they complained when we were forced to forgo a lesson! Their attitude to learning had become positive.

Let me report a few things that surprised me as I 'got started':

- exchange of views with them in conference has helped me understand much better their problems of home and school;
- freed from imposed topics they love to talk and write about their experiences, either with me or with friends;
- they know they can express themselves freely in the rough draft—can confidently 'have a go'—because polishing comes later;
- 'publication' (perhaps helped by typing) boosts their egos, raises their confidence as learners—to see this continually happening is really terrific;
- the way they work at different speeds is healthy—fast writers and slow, writers of long stories and short ones, according to real individual differences;
- I can integrate writing with my previously separate language and spelling lessons—the all-round improvement is quite remarkable.

'I am pleased to say that I found this writing program very stimulating and successful. It's taken away my dislike of teaching writing,' admits Therese Corben.

How I Used to Teach Writing

'Last year I timetabled Writing once a week—Wednesdays 11.15 to 12.30. It was not my favourite subject, nor the children's. But I carefully programmed the topics, sometimes linking with, say, Science (*I Am a Frog*) or Social Studies (*My Best Friend*) and otherwise using imaginative topics. I was always searching for topics.

'I began the lesson with motivational strategies (a picture, object, poem, story, music, etc.). After 10-15 minutes discussion the children would suggest "good words", which I would write on the chalkboard, and then they would go to their seats, open their "Story Book" and start writing. A few times I attempted to get a "draft" written first, but this involved so much extra marking that I did not persist. Talking wasn't banned in my room but it wasn't encouraged.

'The children put up their hands if they wanted a spelling—I would write it in the child's personal dictionary. As stories were completed I would try to read them on the spot, suggesting additions and making corrections. Children who had finished or were waiting for me were asked to draw a picture about their story in a circle I drew underneath. But I always ran out of time and had to collect most of the books for later (and therefore less effective) marking. A special stamp rewarded children who had worked well and I tried to read the best stories to the class.' (*Robyn Platt*)

. . . This description, with variations, would fit most of the writing lessons of previous years in the three schools. Of course, writing in Kindergarten was never considered. Drawing was often considered a time-filler.—*J. T.*

Question: 'Would parent aides be useful in the day-by-day work of a process-conference classroom?'

Answer (by Karen Wade): 'I enlisted parent help when I found I could not meet all the demands for attention that were coming from my Year 1/2 composite class.

'Several parents responded generously. I explained the approach to them and simply asked them to:
(1) listen to the children read their stories,
(2) discuss and gently question, thus helping to extend the stories,
(3) help the typist, with stories that were to be published, by placing correct spelling and punctuation above 'invented spellings'.

'I tried to monitor the parent aides' conferences with the children by occasionally sitting in. Invariably I was happy with what I heard. The parents were sensitive and the children benefited from the individual attention—someone to share their writing with. Moreover I could give more time to the Year 1 children who at that stage needed my help most.

'So, yes, parent aides can be very valuable. I believe that an in-service or demonstration day for interested parents could equip them to be most effective.'

CHAPTER 3

Classroom Organisation

- 'Organisation is demanding!' (P.R.)
- 'As soon as my children become too noisy in a lesson I know something has gone wrong with my planning.' (C.H.)
- 'When children are involved in their work and know what is expected of them, there are few behaviour problems.' (C.B.)
- 'I know things are working well when I'm enjoying teaching as much as the children are enjoying learning.' (R.L.)

Classroom organisation is in many ways very personal. I noticed that every teacher in the Project interacted in an individual way with the children and the physical environment. No two of the 27 classrooms functioned in the same way. Having stressed this, I offer a checklist of some common elements.

Timetabling   *'What is the best time for writing?'*

A.: Try to allocate a regular half-hour daily. Preferably before lunch. Writing is solid mental work, so the children need to be fresh. Some teachers report that the children settle well to writing after a spell of morning physical activity, e.g. first thing, or after recess, of after P.E.

Physical Resources   *'What do I need in the room?'*

A.: See that at least these resources are present:
.. coloured and lead pencils, crayons, textas;
.. rubbers, rulers, scissors, staplers;
.. paper, lined and unlined, in various sizes;
.. reference material, e.g. alphabet chart, dictionaries, captions to pictures, labels naming objects around the room;
.. words listed and displayed, on current class themes;
.. light cardboard for making covers;
.. interesting books in the class library, continually changing.

Grouping   *'Should I arrange the children in groups?'*

A.: See what emerges for you. Many teachers have decided that grouping specifically for this approach is unnecessary. The children sit at their usual places, generally with tables grouped for four or six. They are always able to move around the room when necessary. Certainly there is no call for ability grouping. (But some teachers like to conference with one 'group' each day so as to be sure of seeing everyone each week. This grouping may involve anything from sitting at tables for 'Today's Conference Group' to being called in turn from around the class to come to the teacher's table.)

Parent Aides | *'Should I call on parent aides?'*

A.: Teachers who used parent aides have found them extremely helpful. Only invite them after you and the children have established some working routine. Be sure to brief them on the approach and exactly what you wish them to do. Then, periodically, sit and evaluate with them how the children's work is developing.

Storage | *'How should I store the writing?'*

A.: Each child has a Writing Folder of some kind. It can be kept under the desk, or all the folders can be stored together in a box or tray. Don't let the folders become confusingly overstuffed. Regularly transfer the older work to a central set of file-folders where it is available for reference.

Publications | *'What do I do with the child-authored books?'*

A.: After sharing a newly published 'book' with the class, announce that it is now available for borrowing from the important section of the class library devoted to 'Books by Local Authors' (or whatever title). Applaud attractive covers. Display this stand, shelf or tray prominently. (Some teachers prefer to have a tray of the books on each group of desks.)

Rules | *'What rules should I establish?'*

A.: Establish rules together. Children often have better ideas than yours for saving your sanity. And they are more likely to adhere to rules if they have helped to frame them. The teachers in this project found that devising a new routine takes time and experiment; nor is any routine successful forever. No one is permanently satisfied, so the search for impovement is continuous.

Here are three reports from teachers who had interesting experiences in organising their classrooms. Their insights may be useful to you . . .

How I Organise My Year 2: Robyn Smith

My class of 28 children includes many from non-English-speaking backgrounds. Our writing time is 12.00-12.30 every day.

There's Time to Listen! I begin every session by reading the polished stories completed the previous day, and occasionally I add stories written at home. The children enjoy the variety of topics and especially look forward to hearing their own stories read.

Sometimes they volunteer constructive comments. A number of them are often inspired by original or strongly dramatic pieces to use similar ideas. Occasionally we also invite writers from other classes to read their work to us, and some of our writers visit them.

This brief daily publication-and-response time sets the scene for writing. The children are always keen to start, and their enthusiasm has continued at a high level throughout the year.

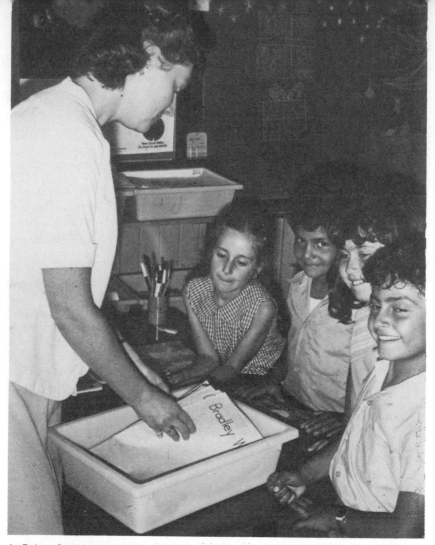

In Robyn Smith's Year 2 class, rough drafts are kept in individual cardboard folders, and are distributed at the beginning of each 'Writing Time'.

There's Time to Organise! I quickly distribute the children's Writing Folders. They contain rough drafts and work being prepared for publication. A table at the front of the room carries two kinds of paper, one suitable for rough drafts, the other for polished work. (We use a great deal of paper, and parents have donated extra supplies.) Lead pencils, coloured pencils and textas are always available in tins on the children's tables. Rubbers can be borrowed from my table when needed.

There's Time to Write! Three main activities can be going on simultaneously: (a) working on a rough draft, (b) talking to me about a piece, (c) preparing writing for publication.
● (a) *Working on the Rough Draft.* The children quickly learned to choose their own topics. Very few now ask me to help. The topics, factual

and imaginative, come in ever-widening variety though I think the underlying content is mostly home, school, family outings, books, films and space. The children whose parents frequently take them on outings have least difficulty in finding topics.

Many of the E.S.L. children have more trouble than the other children with finding topics. This is probably not because they have had fewer experiences but because they need to feel that their experiences will be accepted by the class, especially experiences that are part of cultural happenings the other children don't know about.

Different *forms* of writing are gradually being 'discovered'. All the children had begun by writing stories; then a few attempted poetry. Other forms have since emerged, including captions, rhymes, riddles, singalong jingles, skipping rhymes, news reports and letters. Of course stories and poems remain a strong element. Occasionally poems and parts of favourite stories from books have been copied when original ideas were lacking. I did not discourage this but waited and watched: after a few days the children returned to their own writing with fresh enthusiasm.

● (b) *Talking to the Teacher about the Draft.* Some drafts are completed in one session, others are worked on for several days. The children know they can discuss work-in-progress with one another. They can also come to me at any stage, so I have a steady flow. I encourage the waiting ones to join in discussion of the piece being considered — they seldom have to wait more than a few minutes. (Many talks take less than a minute, but if there is a build-up of writers needing longer talks I don't mind flowing into the early part of the lunch period.)

The individual talks usually involve the content of the story, sentence structure, punctuation marks, setting out the lines of poetry, and writing correct spelling. In this 'parallel class' the ability range is wide, so that while one child looks for frequent help almost sentence by sentence, another races on self-reliantly to complete a book of five chapters with a logical sequence of events.

I firmly believe that by offering the children daily opportunities for individual discussion I reap many advantages. I am able to gauge each child's level early in the year and thereafter closely follow progress. Difficulties are dealt with at the moment of need. I get to know intimately every child's background and interests. So I am able to give help and praise to every writer *individually* two or three times a week.

● (c) *Preparing Writing for Publication.* The child chooses from several drafts the one he or she wishes to publish. Occasionally I demur on grounds of unacceptable language or damaging reference to someone — which obliges me to discuss my 'censorship' role with the writer, *and* amendments or a resort to a different draft.

In the interests of encouraging self-reliance, I try to keep my help with editing to a minimum. If I think a child is capable of editing most of the work or expanding the ideas, I tactfully suggest that he or she do so.

When editing is finished, the rough draft is usually copied by the child onto foolscap pages. The children show pride in this work; I rarely have to mention the importance of clear legible handwriting. Their polishing is completed with care. Most illustration is imaginative, drawn with textas, and it is usually accompanied by thoughtful captions. The lengthier pieces of writing are typed by volunteer mothers and then made into books by the writer, with illustrations. The shorter pieces are displayed on eye-level boards for reading by the class. I find time each day to send them to read these 'latest stories' for themselves and to comment to one another. After a short time the board stories are taken down and placed in each writer's individual 'book'.

Time to Evaluate! My Year 2 children say, 'Writing is top!' I can only add, 'This is easily the most successful approach to writing I have tried.'

How I Organise My Year 2: Carolyn Bowman

The organisation of this class of 12 girls and 15 boys for writing tended to 'happen'; it was not preconceived and imposed. The writing period quickly attained popularity: 'Is it story time yet?' they would clamour. Interest in one another's stories has continued to run high, accompanied by emulation of themes, topics, even characters — the Fruit People, for instance, swept through the classroom, with Mr Orange, Miss Apple, the Banana children and others enacting great adventures.

Freedom and Variety. The children can move around freely. Mostly they write at their own desks but may go to other desks or write on the floor. Some sit next to a friend to write, or talk about, or read the story. Their comments to each other often bring home to me the depth of their thinking about the story and characters. Some children are self-motivated and don't feel a need for talking with peers; absorbed, they only come to me for a conference when the story is finished. Of course I wish there were more like that! I have to be tolerant of a certain noise level from the talkers — and at times I check those who become too noisy.

The Writing Folder. Current and recently completed draft stories are kept in the child's personal Folder, all of them dated. The children often re-read their stories. I feel this is important, as is also the fact that they sometimes take a past story and revise it. Sara goes further; after re-reading her stories she will often write another story using a character she considered she has used successfully. Her confidence grows by leaning on a past success. As the Folder fills, the older stories are transferred to the child's file-folder in a class box, which is accessible for reading.

The inside-cover of the Folder carries a checklist of achieved writing skills, e.g.

Things I Can Do
  .. use full stops at end of sentence
  .. use capital letters at beginning
  .. use capitals for people and places (see 'My Trip to Canberra')
  .. use 'were' in right place ('we were excited')
  .. use speech marks (see my book 'Mr. Chatterbox').

The back cover of the Folder carries a list of topics the children may write about. I ask them to keep adding topics whenever they think of them. Sometimes I gather into a group any children who currently express dif-

Great Stories (by Robyn Smith's Year 2)
There was knock at the door. Who is it?
It could be a robber or the baker.
It could be a monster.
It might be a dragon.
"Open the door dear, it's me."
"Who's me?"
"Dad of course."

Ruth

Home is a good place.
Home you know is a good, good place.
I like home.

Michelle

I like to do pictures. I like to do Lebanese dancing.
I like to do stories too. I like to do a lot of things.
I like to do things at school. The work I do is nice.
I like it. I like to do Lebanese things at home.
I like to do a lot of things. I like to do work.
I like to do maths too. I like to go to school.

Sam (Lebanese)

Outer Space
   In the Year 1987, Nasa launched the last of America's Deep Space
Probes and a great miss happened. I got blown out of my projector·
ray into an orbit that froze my light seaport systems and sent me to
Mars 500 years later. I was found by the Martians in that century.
They melted the ice I was in and aimed me at Jupiter. It was a bad
aim too. Between Mars and Jupiter there were astronoids. I dodged
the astronoids. I went right past Jupiter. Then I went past Saturn.
Then I went past Uranus and Neptune and landed on Pluto. The
temperature on Pluto was 1,000,000 degrees below freezing. It was so
cold I had to leave. I WENT BACK TO EARTH!

Bradley

ficulty in finding a topic. We discuss possibilities, and they add the ones
that appeal to them.

Conferences. Time is so short! It is difficult to see enough of the children
individually. Some want my attention to hear their stories at every turn of
the page. Fortunately others, like Carla, can write cheerfully for weeks
without coming to see me. She filled an exercise book with 'Fruit People'
before I was invited to read the first chapter. But in general I need to keep
a check so that no child is overlooked: once a week I move around the room
to talk with those who haven't come to see me. They know I'll be coming,
and that I'm in touch with their work.

Carolyn Bowman discusses with 7 year old Toula how the author of this commercial book used speech marks.

I keep a record of each long talk I have with a child; this will usually be about a story that's to be published. My Record Folder has become an important record of progress and I refer to it often. I can sometimes jot down points during the conference but mostly I do this immediately afterwards. For example, I note the main things discussed, the skills that are being used well, those that are only beginning to be used, major shifts in thinking (a new interest, say in reading or science, or the first appearance of a new mode such as an imaginative story or a letter), or specific formal difficulties with sentence structure, tense, spelling, sequencing, etc.

Publication. In a conference, the child chooses for publication his or her best story out of the last four and gives some reasons for the choice. The limit is necessary in a class which produces so much writing. These children are at once 'learning to write by writing' (a quantity) and deliberating with the teacher on what makes writing appealing (quality).

Together we work through the story to make sure its sequence and meaning are clear. I don't write on the child's story but encourage the child to make changes in the light of our talk. If I feel there is a need, I write on a piece of paper that is mine and invite the child to copy it into his or her story. Our final check is on punctuation and spelling and I always point out one new thing that I perceive is within the child's grasp. It is added to the list in the child's Folder.

When the story has been sufficiently edited, the child can elect to write it out or have it typed by a volunteer mother. From one story to the next, this decision can vary. The child decides on the page sequence and layout and then finally does the illustrating.

Reading the Stories. The children are eager to read their stories aloud to anyone. I reward those who have worked particularly hard by sending them to read to other classes. I also encourage as much reading aloud as possible during waiting time or any free time. This is particularly valuable for E.S.L. children. Vladimir, a Yugoslav boy, on re-reading a story in which he had written, 'Mr. Hairy with no clothes on', changed to 'Mr. Hairy has no clothes on'. I believe his sense of English structures has improved greatly *through writing*, giving him new confidence orally.

Improvements Next Year. My kind of classroom organisation has worked quite well this year, but I will be trying to improve next year, especially in (1) finding more time for each child to talk about his or her stories; (2) discerning the writing skills that need discussion; (3) working with the one or two children who need a great deal of the teacher's help in completing a task. However, these considerations do not overshadow the confidence and enthusiasm that nearly all my children have shown this year in 'Story Time'.

How I Organise My Kindergarten Class: Lurline Grime

Our 'Story Writing' is a daily event, from 10.30 till recess at 11.00. My 23 typically 'egocentric' five year olds quickly grew to look forward to it because they all found they could 'write' something. Nearly all have made rapid progress, and there has been a general sense of being involved in mastering an important ability.

The Classroom at Work. Crayons, lead pencils and coloured pencils are available. The children write mainly on foolscap-size sheets and staple two or more sheets together if they need to. A child is chosen each day to go around the groups of tables date-stamping everyone's work.

I now work with one group each day. This was difficult to establish as so many children wanted to show me their work the moment they finished it. I told them I was being swamped and encouraged them to talk and work with one another — which they are now doing well.

These beginning writers seem to need to complete each piece of work in a single session. Most are not interested in resuming unfinished work at a later date. Within the session they spend varying amounts of time on their writing/drawing, some finishing quickly, others using the whole period. I allow the early finishers to conference with others, read the piece to others or choose a language game that interests them (preferably a self-corrective one) or a book. They leave their completed stories on their tables at the end of the period knowing I will read them.

The children in Lurline Grime's Kindergarten know they can move to another activity when they have finished writing.

Starting Them Writing for Themselves. To present this end-of-year picture of our classroom organisation is to overlook the process — the struggle! — needed to reach our current point of enthusiasm and (considering the children's age) self-reliance.

Our first step in 'Story Writing' was to look at ways to tell a story: (1) orally, (2) in pictures, (3) in written or printed words. We discussed each and regularly examined the books in the class library, noticing that some tell stories solely through pictures, others through pictures *and* words. The children found that they could deduce a story from pictures even when they couldn't read the words; also, I did a lot of reading aloud to them and showed related pictures. The importance of all this reading, looking and sharing through discussion can't be emphasised too much.

At first the children began 'writing' by drawing a picture. I tried to scribe the story of the picture for each of them but soon found this took a great amount of time. It was at this point that I divided the class into groups so that I could work with just one group each day. This meant that I had to persuade the others to work on their own, discussing with someone *and starting to write for themselves.*

Within 'today's group' I asked the children to draw and then write as much as they could, and if need be I would finish the story for them. The first efforts often included writing any sounds or numerals they knew, whether related to their stories or not. In conference they would point and tell me the story, which I would write in 'grown-up writing'. I was careful never to give them the impression that I thought their 'writing' was wrong. Children at this stage should always feel that *what they present is entirely acceptable*. This gives them confidence to continue writing and not start saying, 'I can't write. I don't know how'.

I soon introduced an alphabet chart showing upper and lower case letters. The usual weather and seasons charts were also on display together with names of days of the week, colours and shapes, and the children's names, all treated during appropriate lessons. After a while the children began making use of these for their stories. Never before have I known a kindergarten class so aware of the print around the room. At the same time they began to show interest in the *sounds* and *shapes* of words. I seized every opportunity to discuss phonic aspects of words in use, without feeling a need for systematic phonics drill. Games such as 'I spy' and finding pictures beginning with the same sound became meaningful to them.

As they became involved with the sounding out of words, I explained and encouraged 'invented spelling': 'Write whatever sound you think is in a word, or the sound you hear when you say the word aloud'. They helped one another a lot at this stage, readily asking questions: 'How do you write "R"?' 'How does "aeroplane" start?' 'Does this [pointing to a letter in a name on the desk] say "M"?' I continued for a time to write their stories in 'grown-up writing' but only after they had read the 'writing' to me, touching the 'words' as they read them. This way, they often discovered the omission of words or the insertion of sounds that weren't necessary in their words — it was the beginning of editing for them. Again, to ensure I gave no impression that I thought their writing was wrong, I explained that I needed to use my writing because I couldn't always read theirs, just as they couldn't always read mine.

These young ones show less interest in 'publication' than do children in Years 1 and 2. Their great interest is in 'doing' the writing. Only those who are reading well will sometimes ask for their work to be published.

Writing before Reading

At 4 years and 9 months Alison entered a kindergarten class of writers on her first day of school. A few weeks later she solemnly presented to her mother a page of 'writing' of the 'sea waves' type.

'That's good,' said her mother. 'Will you read it to me?'

'Don't be silly, Mummy,' said Alison. '*You* know how to read. But I'm only little. I can only write yet.'

CHAPTER 4

The Conference

The 'conference' is—what? It is a talk between a teacher and a child or group of children about their work. It is time set aside for that purpose. It is an incomparable means of individualising the teaching-learning relationship. And though in one sense it is simply 'a talk', it is also, for the teacher, an art—chiefly the art of drawing forth ideas and fostering thinking, by asking questions.

Some teachers find the word 'conference' stilted; they prefer to use 'talk' or 'discussion'. But most teachers overcome the initial awkwardness and find the term useful. Children respond readily to, 'Are you ready for a conference on that piece yet?' Perhaps they catch a suggestion that this is no passing chat but a one-to-one consultation that regards the piece of writing as a significant creation.

> • 'At the core of the conference is a teacher asking a child to teach her about the subject. The aim is to foster a bursting desire to inform. So the teacher never implies a greater knowledge of this topic than the child possesses, nor treats the child as an inferior learner. We are in the business of helping children to value what they know. Ideally, the poorer the writing the greater interest the teacher will show in it—or rather in what it might become.' —*Donald H. Graves*

The Many Uses of the Writing Conference

Conferences may take a few seconds or several minutes or more than ten minutes. Such different times point to many different uses. This is not surprising since a conference can be concerned with *any* aspect of a child's (or group's) involvement in the writing process, all the way from topic-choosing through drafting and editing to preparing polished work for publication. The possible range of conferences is worth indicating:

- *'a few seconds' of conference:* e.g. Simply answering a child's question ('Does carrot have two Rs?'). A teacher sitting with a group and mainly working with one child can be considered to 'conference' with another by responding to a question.
- *'several minutes' of conference:* e.g. Listening to the first part of a piece and helping the child to move on ('What happened then?' 'How did you feel?'); or helping the child to improve a sequence ('What happened *between* your bike crashing and your arrival home?').
- *'more than ten minutes' of conference:* e.g. Helping a child through an emotional crisis brought on by a frustration with writing (by working to solve the writing problem); or helping with the final polishing and preparation of a piece for publication. (N.B. These longer conferences may take place in the writing period, but heavy demands on the teacher's attention may cause postponement to a later time in the day, such as a free reading time or even part of the lunch period.)

Points to Remember in the Conference

If a reader feels at all anxious about 'conferencing', rest assured that after some awkwardness a sense of confidence will grow. What is aimed at is a *one-to-one interaction in which the teacher fosters self-learning by the child*. The teacher is advised to . . .

.. play a low-key role, not dominating or talking too much;
.. show interest in what the child is trying to express;
.. get to know as many of the child's interests as possible;
.. be aware of the child's strengths and weaknesses in writing;
.. leave the pencil in the child's hand (for additions, etc.);
.. develop the art of questioning; instead of telling what to do, use questions to move the child to find answers;
.. in short, *be positive at all times*.

The Kinds of Questions Teachers Ask in Conference

The teacher's questions or responses are as specific as possible:
.. 'Please read me your story.'
.. 'What part do you like best? . . . Why?'
.. 'What happened after *this*?' 'How did you *feel*?'
.. 'As reader, I don't follow this part. Can you explain . . .?'
.. 'Is there a part you aren't happy with? . . . Why?'
.. 'What can you do to make this beginning of your draft better?'
.. 'What's the most important thing you're saying in this piece?'
.. 'Have you checked this by reading it to a friend?'
.. 'What words do you think you've used best?'
.. 'Can you think of a different way to say this?'
.. 'The words on the page don't tell me that. How could you write it to let the reader know?'
.. 'How did you end your last piece? Is this different?'

'What do you want this part to say?' Marilyn Rigg asks 6 year old Sarah.

In a conference the teacher must resist the adult temptation to tell the child what to do. Patience and skilful questioning are needed in helping the child to move forward.

In Conference (1): Steven Learns to Insert Sentences

Steven handed me his story. 'For publishing,' he said.

'Have you read it to a friend?' I asked.

'Yes, but he's dopey. He says it's muddled up.'

'Read it to me,' I said . . . It confused me too. In fact I only realised it was about a car race when he announced that 'Number 10 won'. So I asked him to tell me the story without looking at the words.

'Well, they were all lined up at the edge of the road —'

'Wait,' I said. 'Where is that part in the story?'

Irritated, he looked, then said, 'I haven't wrote that yet.'

'Well, where would you write it so the reader knows your story is about a car race?'

He picked up his pencil and wrote the sentence — at the end! Into my impatient mind flashed the uncharitable thought, 'No, dimwit, write it at the beginning.' But I managed to stay silent . . . When he finished, I asked him to read it back.

When he did so he said, 'That's not right.' Then reluctantly, 'That sentence doesn't make sense there.'

'Do you know what you can do about it?'

'I could write it up there' — pointing to the top of the page. 'M-m-m, but I don't have enough room.'

'What else could you do?' I asked, dying to tell him.

After what seemed an age, 'I could draw a line to there.'

'Good, then I'd know you wanted that sentence up there.'

He drew a line from the sentence to the top of the page and for good measure wrote, 'PUT HERE.'

I congratulated him. Steven had learnt an important editing skill which he has used several times since. I congratulated myself too — on holding my tongue and allowing him to make the discovery. On the other hand, if he had grown frustrated, finding the 'block' insurmountable, I would have discussed expedients that I and others use in such a situation . . . The conference had taken 15 minutes. I noted his achievement in my record book. And he made a note too, in the 'Things I Have Learned' section of his writing folder. Then he place the story in the container for the typist. (*J.T.*)

In Conference (2): Merilyn Learns to Cross Out and Add

Five year old Merilyn had written a story about Christmas:

Mary is standing

up. Two flash

es came in

in the sky.

A fairy said, "Mary

here is your

crown."

Reading it to me, she became confused when she reached 'FASH' on one line and 'aS' on the next. She had read 'flashes' when she looked at 'FASH' then didn't know what to read for 'aS'. So I asked her to read the piece again and touch each word as she did so.

After several attempts, she pointed to the 'aS' in the third line and said, 'That part should be up there' (touching 'FASH').

'How could you put it up there?'

'I could write it there.' And she wrote an 'a' after 'FASH', then crossed out the 'a' in the third line.

Reading the story again, she stopped at 'FASHa', picked up her pencil and confidently added an 'S'.

What Teachers Say about the Conference

- 'In the conference the children see me more as a friend than as a teacher. They talk more readily to me.' — *Linda Mein*
- 'You must not try to achieve for them. Be encouraging and you'll find that the conference is always a means of helping them to progress at their own rate.' — *Robyn Legge*
- 'I find the most difficult part is resisting the adult temptation to tell a child what to do or at least make leading suggestions. With practice I now feel more confident about when to question and when to leave a problem with the child. I continually remind myself how I'd feel if I were that child.' — *Judy Antoniolli*
- 'The children are more familiar with the conference now and know that it is their time. They are giving more of themselves and attempting more.' — *Liz Marshall*
- 'The children now realise that sometimes one child's conference will take quite some time; so they wait, knowing that they will in turn get all my individual attention. While they wait they enjoy conferencing with one another.' — *Robyn Platt*
- 'The conference is the key to the teaching/learning aspect in this writing program. You become more aware of the strengths and weaknesses of individual children and the progress that each child can make at any one time. It is the means of truly individualising learning.' — *Jim Findlay*

She continued reading, but now also touching the words. After reading *'came in'* distinctly as two words for 'CAMiN' she looked at the fourth line, stopped, and crossed out the 'iN'. 'I'm silly,' she said, 'I wrote *in* two times.'

She read the piece several times, touching the words to check she was right, then announced with satisfaction,'There, finished!'

As her text shows, she had already used bracketing as a way of crossing out, but today she had learnt that she can also cross out and make additions. She had perceived too that touching words helps her to see them. When she is ready she will begin to use spacing between words where at present she only spaces between sentences. She has illustrated the typed version of her story (which is in conventional spelling) and proudly reads it to anyone who will listen. (*J. T.*)

In Conference (3): Gavin Learns to Reduce His 'And Thens . . .'

One conference is seldom enough when the child is preparing a long story for publication. In a *first conference* I ask the writer to read it so that I get the general meaning. We then usually go through it a second time and the child usually notices words left out or not needed. The pencil is in the child's hand, not mine, for making additions or crossings-out.

I often ask, 'Which is your best part?' Then, 'Is there a part you aren't happy about?' They always know! It may be unclear, clumsy, ambiguous or simply incomplete. We discuss it, I asking specific questions and resisting the temptation to *tell*, and the child answering or making fresh suggestions. After a further reading we leave it for the day.

While waiting for her second conference, 7 year old Helen listens to the story Bahia has just drafted.

While waiting for a *second conference* the child can revise, or begin a new story, or read or illustrate other stories, or help other writers. At this conference we usually go carefully page by page, still focusing on meaning. When I'm satisfied the meaning is clear for the reader I shift the focus to punctuation and spelling. In effect I now ask: 'Have you made use, for the reader's benefit, of the punctuation and spelling you know?' (Again I resist temptation to take these 'mechanics' out of the child's hands by inserting what is obvious from my adult level.)

Finally, I am usually able to perceive, infer or intuit some new aspect of the work which the child is ready to learn. For instance, seven year old Gavin had written an interesting story which we had been through several times and at last I focused attention on his numerous 'and thens'.

We decided to place a plastic counter (from the previous Maths lesson) over every 'and then' on the first page. He read the story through carefully aloud removing a counter when he decided the 'and then' was necessary to maintain meaning. When he finished reading the page he simply removed the remaining counters and crossed out the unnecessary 'and thens'. From the fourth page he worked on the 'and thens' confidently without the counters. Of course I could have suggested other phrasings but I knew he had many years ahead in which to make his own discoveries.

Gavin's long story — six quarto pages — needed three conferences. He certainly improved on his first draft. I congratulated him and accepted it for publication — by typing which would edit its 'invented spellings' and its frequent dialogue into conventional 'edited English'. (*J. T.*)

In Conference (4): Kindergarten Children Gain Confidence

The conference has been valuable to me as a splendid means of getting to know my 28 children *individually*; it has been no less valuable to them because, although they thought they couldn't write a 'proper' story, they now know that they can make a confident attempt which their teacher praises. Moreover they spontaneously 'conference' with one another, and though this sometimes produces similar stories within groups, they never copy exactly and seem rather to be intent on being mutually supportive.

The children look forward to this time to talk with me. Each knows that I am there just for him or her. Let me give four examples . . .

Ashley has found, through writing, a means of expression needed by a child who is at present rather reserved in oral situations. He shows me his stories of things he does at home, 'reading' the letter symbols he is making and explaining points in answer to my questions.

Fiona has quickly moved from stereotyped sentences ('I can see Mum', 'I went to the shop') to rows and rows of letters which as yet have no real word formation but which she translates into meaningful sentences that explain her detailed and beautiful drawings. She enjoys reading to me.

Faihaa, who is Lebanese, came to our class a couple of months ago with no English. At first she drew objects for which I wrote words, e.g. apple, car, girl. Now she is speaking simple sentences, drawing more meaningful pictures and 'writing' stories about them, having begun by using letters

'Why do you think this story should be published, Peter?' asks Sue Wyndham.

Judy Harris and 6 year old Kerry, in conference, prepare a rough draft for publication.

from her own name. The conference enables me to encourage her to speak and I gauge her current language needs.

Matthew shows advanced reading and spelling skills. In the conference my main aim is to extend him with questions . . . Thus with each child I am able to work at the individual level. (*Sue Wyndham*)

In Conference (5): Judy Harris Tells What Usually Happens

Each week I give to my 31 Year 1 children a blank booklet of stapled computer paper. They might write a short story each day or a long one that takes the whole week. While they are working on these, most of my time is spent in individual conferences about the previous week's stories which the children have chosen for publication. *Here are the sorts of things I discuss:*

(1) I show my interest: 'Why did you write about this?' 'How do you know so much about . . .?' 'Tell me more about . . .?'

(2) I ask the child to read the story. If there is a confusing part, I re-read it and say, 'Tell me that, in your words.'

(3) Sequence is important. They often leave things out, assuming that readers know; so I ask, 'Who did that?' 'What happened next?'

(4) Sometimes I ask them to consult references around the room — words, charts, relevant books.

(5) I teach 'conventions' in context (mainly when polishing for publication) by questioning about things the child knows, e.g. where a capital

or fullstop is needed. Finally, I insert some things myself with the explanation that the typist needs these for the published form. But if the child, not the typist, is going to write the final published form then I insert spelling and punctuation for the child to copy, explaining that this is necessary for the readers.

(6) I question about title, page-layout, and pictures that will make the 'book' more attractive.

(7) When a story confuses me, I've learnt to ask, 'Which part is best? . . . Why?' This brings identification of the theme. We can work from there. Sometimes the child can start again, using this as the 'lead' and writing on from it.

(8) Every conference is different, for each child has a unique story and an individual grasp of skills. At the same time, every conference is similar in that it brings me close to a child's inner world, enables me to sense strengths and needs, and suggests the next 'teaching point' that will chime in with the onward flow of the child's learning. (*Judy Harris*)

Every Writer Needs a Little Green Man

'O.K.,' said Ben. 'I'll try it out on the Little Green Man.'

He went back to his table to clarify and expand his story 'with a definite reader in mind'.

This reader is a visitor from Mars, no less. He turned up in our classroom one morning when I spontaneously and a little testily said, 'Look, you can't expect a reader to *know* — you've got to *tell* him. Now, if I was a Little Green Man from Mars, I wouldn't know what you were talking about.'

The children welcomed him! . . . They now regularly use this gimmick in the cooperative peer conferences that often take place.

CHAPTER 5

The Writing Time

The preceding chapters have given the reader an overview of the process-conference classroom in action, but now a good deal of detail needs to be filled in. To do this we must divide the writing process into a number of stages; but in doing so let us remember that a living 'process' is by definition continuous. The following 'stages' tend in practice to flow into one another in these classes' 'writing time' — usually half an hour every day.

1. Topic Choice
2. Drawing
3. Draft Writing (using 'invented spelling')
4. Preparing for Publication

1. Topic Choice

For too long we teachers have underestimated children's desire to write and *their ability to find topics for themselves*. We assumed that 'teaching writing' meant assigning topics and compelling children to write about them. Not that we haven't been conscientious! We've constantly searched for 'good and exciting topics' in the belief that 'motivation' of the writing has depended heavily on our choice.

The 27 teachers in this Project have verified two principles: first, that even small children can themselves find topics to write about (nearly all the time); second, that children write best, and develop most rapidly as writers, when they write on topics they care about. I have continually been thrilled at the surprising range of topics chosen by the children.

All the teachers offered their classes the utmost freedom of topic choice. Here are snippets from their reports . . .

(a) Free Choice

● **'A Free Interaction of Ideas': Judy Harris.** 'This is a non-directed, far from formal approach. There is a buzz of voices, a free flow of thought, an interaction of ideas which gives the writing session an air of excitement as every child individually chooses, interprets and presents his or her topic.' (*Year 1 class*)

● **'Many Things Spark Off Our Writing': Wendy Goebel.** 'The visit to school of a blind man, alarm at a bushfire right beside the school, the technicalities of making an Easter basket, favourite songs, personal tastes in food, fear of the dark and nightmares, frustrations caused by younger brothers and sisters — these are but a few of the subjects my children have *chosen* to write about. We also have lively and often philosophical[1] discussions at least once and sometimes two or three times a day, whenever I find children who are bursting to tell of experiences, thoughts and fears. This sparks off writing . . .' (*Year 2 class*)

---

[1] Anyone who doubts that small children are capable of engagement in philosophical discussion should consult *Philosophy and the Young Child* by Gareth B. Matthews (Harvard University Press, 1981). He shows that they enjoy and profit from such discussion. — *Ed.*

● **'Ideas Catch on in This Class': Janeen Bartlett.** 'Because my children are keen to listen to stories and the good readers borrow books from the library, they derive many writing themes from these sources. The *Mr Men Series*, for instance, launched a wide range of writing, some of it being rewriting from memory in their own words, but more of it making use of a Mr Tickle or Mr Mischief original adventure stories. Other topics include TV series (*The Duke Boys, Flash Gordon*), cars and bikes, cicadas, flowers, springtime, dinosaurs . . . Ideas catch on in this class. When the children realised I was pregnant, suddenly a wide variety of people and animals met, fell in love, got married and had babies! . . . No one is ever stumped for topics now they have gained confidence as writers. They are very supportive of one another. My difficulty is stopping them.' (*Year 1 class*)

● **'Ideas from the Classroom Environment': Linda Mein.** 'The classroom environment is an important source of ideas and topics in Kindergarten. Realising this I now think carefully about what I put up . . . I've decided not to give the children their own *Breakthrough to Literacy* folders because I've found they write better stories without it. I do keep the teacher's stand at the back of the room with only the words on it that I've treated, and some of these are used in stories, but the children make much more use of words from the chalkboard where I write items from daily work ("There are 10 boys in our class today," etc.). They often copy the colour words from above the board. The Alphabet Chart, with a word for each sound, is popular with them, and the better readers make use of our Art and Craft signs. The children like me to consult them about anything I put up and they usually suggest things I should add . . . Girls often write about their friends in the class, but the boys' topics tend to be trucks, racing cars, aeroplanes, rockets, ghosts, and Batman.'

(b) When Children Need Some Help

Adults occasionally experience 'writer's block' when 'I just can't think of anything to write about' — and so do children. At such times the teacher can *assist* topic-choice without needing to impose a topic. Here are some examples from teachers who have done this within a framework of completely free choice:

● **'Many Ways to Help': Judy Harris.** 'While the main source of topics is the children's own experiences and the daily interaction of their ideas about them, I keep suggestions available for anyone who is temporarily stuck for a topic:

.. we regularly brainstorm ideas for our 'Good Story Topics' Chart and add bright ideas as they arise;
.. we keep a 'Story Box' of assorted items — shells, seeds, spectacles, an alarm clock, etc. — to stir the imagination and the senses;
.. we keep a 'Picture File', chiefly of magazine cuttings which the children bring from home.

I direct any child with a topic problem to the Chart, the Box or the File before we have a conference together.' (*Year 1 class*)

'Look, I've finished my poem, Mrs Wade. Can I read it to you now?' asks 7 year old Julie.

- **'Children Need Literary Models': Karen Wade.** 'Poetry doesn't just happen. The teacher must expose children to models of poetry — and other modes of expression. I present poems, plays, short stories, fairytales, novels, factual reports, newspaper articles, advertisements, etc. My immediate motive is always the enjoyment or interest of the piece, but the children often experiment with these forms.

'Working hand in hand with such "input sessions" are the "sharing sessions" that conclude our daily writing periods: several children read out their writing, in draft or published form, and the class comments. Often I focus attention on a mode not used yet by some of them (a poem or play, perhaps) and I may write a part on the board. This gives them the idea, "If Bill can do that, I sure can" or "I'll try that and ask Bill to help me." ' (*Composite Years 1/2 class*)

- **'A Balanced Diet Produces Healthy Writing': Wendy Goebel.** 'Writing seems to feed on the input given to children. Reading to them, talking with them, and exposing them to worthwhile experiences — this is the food for their thinking and writing. The more balanced the diet the healthier the writing . . . Last week we arrived back from an excursion with ten minutes to spare before hometime. I went to get a cup of coffee and when I returned, *every* child was immersed in writing, all without one word from me. Despite a daily period of writing they now deem it a great privilege to be allowed to write in any free time they have. I believe this love they have for writing has been helped by the fact that I sometimes write with them and read them what I have written—pieces about our common experiences or my homelife or earlier life.' (*Year 2 class*)

(c) Free Choice within a Prescribed General Subject

Occasionally a teacher assigned a general subject area but offered free topic choice *within* it. For example, 'As part of Social Studies I asked my Year 2 to write about Captain Cook after we had treated his exploits and visited the Cook Museum on Botany Bay. The diversity of both form and content in what they wrote stunned me—autobiography, biography, reports, even a poem, with some concentrating on the seatrip, others on the landing and others on the artefacts and memorials in the Museum. Each child was confidently in control of the writing of his or her choice even though I prescribed the broad subject.' (*Carolyn Bowman*)

(d) A Need to Write Every Day

'Constant practice is necessary in developing any skill. It is good that this is at last being recognised for the complex skill of writing, as it has always been for reading and maths. *Every child needs a period of writing every day.* This regularity will keep the quest for topics in the forefront of the child's mind—though at times he or she will need some help from the teacher.' (*Ruth Staples: Year 2 class*)

Five year old Joanne has begun to read and is keen to publish her writing. However, Fiona Powning has observed that children not yet reading are satisfied to simply write/draw their pieces and not publish them.

(e) Writing Can Facilitate Integration

'We know that many topics for writing arise out of a class's activities in reading, talking and engaging in "experiences". So how can the class's half-hour a day of "writing time" be kept in a separate pigeonhole? Why shouldn't it be extended to encompass or overlap "reading time", "discussion time" and "experience time" (i.e. excursions, observing, Science or Social Studies investigations)? In other words, writing regarded as a significant act of original thinking/self-expression/communication, needs to be treated as part—and often the culminating part—of "integrated learning". A child writing willingly is responding, integrating, making much of the experience of life. Which is what the best learning is supposed to be all about!' (*Robyn Legge: Year 1 class*)

---

2. Drawing

'Does drawing really help writing? I'm afraid it may waste time.'

It certainly helps young writers. We've long overlooked its importance to them as a manageable means of clarifying and representing ideas. They enjoy 'telling' stories through their drawings. In fact drawing, along with what we adults gratuitously term the 'scribble'[2] or 'scrawl' of a young child, needs to be regarded as an integral part of the process of that child's rudimentary writing.

'It's a Springboard into Writing': Fiona Powning

My class of young kinders had little knowledge of sound-symbols but were willing to attempt writing *their* way—which for many of them meant happily 'drawing a story' and telling me about it. A few also 'scribbled' under the drawing and some wrote apparently random letters, e.g. 'a b B Λ R': *but*, if asked, every child could 'read' these 'writings'. From the moment I legitimised drawing in our 'writing time', more detail appeared and the topics began changing significantly, becoming less oriented to self and family and more imaginative and interesting to the other children.

As the year passed they moved more towards writing, though drawings have remained an integral part of the writing process. Moreover they love to read their published stories to one another and are thus learning to read through their writing. I'm thrilled at what they can do.

'Drawing, Writing and a Role for Scribing': Linda Mein

Before this Project, I used to scribe every word for every child in 'story time'. I didn't realise that Kindergarten children can attempt to write for themselves. At the beginning of the year these very young children when asked to write in 'writing time' were all willing to draw and to tell extremely detailed stories about their drawings. As my record, I would write each story in small print at the top of the page, explaining that this 'grown-up writing' would help me to remember it. But if they expressed a wish to 'read' it too, I would do large printing at the bottom. This scribing

---

[2] An illuminating study of children's progression 'from scribble to script' is Marie Clay's *What Did I Write?* (Heinemann Education, Auckland, 1975).

became an important source of *reading* for them, as they often referred back to it in their 'Story Book' (held together by curtain rings which open to take continual additions). They also referred back to it to copy the spelling of key words when they were writing.

As the children began to write for themselves some became frustrated and tired because their writing was slow and laboured. So I suggested they write what they could and I would scribe the rest. This has encouraged them to launch into more involved stories. Because they like to finish a story in a session, my scribing is a help. Next year, no doubt, they will be more inclined to work on the same story over a couple of sessions, and then scribing will no longer be needed.

'Drawing Helped These Four Young Children': Jan Turbill

William, Megan, Michael and Darren are examples of Kindergarten children whom I have seen *assisted towards writing by teachers who encouraged them to draw*. The teacher's role is significant, first, in supporting the child's efforts to draw-write while accepting all attempts to spell; and, second, in serving as a responsive listener who asks questions that help the child to think out the moves in the story.

William had drawn a monster bird that had frightened his sister in the middle of the night. His teacher's questions prompted him to go back to the drawing and make additions. Later, he brought her the drawing and said excitedly, 'Look, I didn't know it was going to rain until I drawed it!' Here was a five year old's version of novelist E. M. Forster's famous dictum, 'How can I know what I think till I've written it down?' In this case, drawing was the agent of creativity.

Megan always drew pictures of a pretty little girl with pigtails. Her latest showed the girl against a background of trees, flowers and a lake with three smiling purple fish. She eagerly answered questions from her teacher.

'And why are your fish smiling?'

'Cos they like the little girl.'

'What story are you going to write?'

'A little girl was walking happily in the woods one day. She was happy because the fishies smiled at her.'

The process of drawing (with some talk to others) had helped her formulate her story; it was a rehearsal for the 'writing'. In telling the story to the teacher she changed her language from a spoken to a written register. (The teacher encouraged her to try to write it for publication and undertook to finish it by scribing if Megan grew tired of writing what was, for a five year old, a long story.)

Michael drew a sequence of events on the page, a violent conflict between a ghost and a giant at a hospital. It looked a mess to his teacher but she certainly didn't say so; instead she asked questions — and received clear explanations. Unlike Megan he didn't ask his teacher to scribe for him. Why should he? 'You can *see* the story,' he said confidently. The teacher did not press him. She judged that his story-sequencing was developing. Soon the example of the other children writing would cause him to want to write too.

Drawing is part of the writing process of beginning writers. The drawing is a means of collecting and expressing thoughts.

Darren showed an even more advanced grasp of logical sequence, drawing each event on a separate page. He began almost at once to write an occasional letter or two on the top of each picture, these being letters from his own and his sisters' names. He had no trouble 'reading' them as his story.

'Drawing Can Also Help a 7 Year Old': Robyn Platt

While the amount of drawing soon decreases — probably in the second half of Year 1 for most children — and the amount of writing increases, the usefulness of drawing should not be limited to 5-6 years olds. Take, for instance, 7 year old Christopher, a relatively confident writer. When he brought me his three-chapter story, *The Dog Lost in Space*, it was obvious that he was as lost in narrative confusion as the dog was in space. Questions failed to help him unravel a sequence, so I asked him to draw the events, cartoon-style.

He did so happily, with great detail and sound effects. At last he could *see* the events. He turned confidently to revising chapter three and *continually referred to the drawing as he wrote.* The story-line became clear. Drawing had played a crucial role in helping this boy to revise.

Invented Spelling Explained

Children don't need to be taught to read before we allow them to write. They seem to know this instinctively. If we ask them to 'Write!' before they are given any writing instruction, they gravely *do something* with crayon, pen or pencil, even if it appears to be 'scribble' or if it is a drawing without any attempt at words. But we should take these expressions seriously as establishing each child's readiness-point for individualised classroom writing.

In the past, many attempts have been made to devise a way to move children from that readiness-point into regular writing. The conference approach chooses 'invented spelling' as the most natural possible way. A researcher, Donald H. Graves, has found that 'a child who knows six sound-symbol relationships (usually consonants) can begin to write'. Many children already know more than that, and those who don't are happy to use any symbols they do know until they become aware of the standard sound-symbol system.

● The teacher simply asks the child to write whatever sounds he or she hears in a word (or remembers having seen in a spelling).

● Children *tend* to begin their inventing of spelling by writing only the first consonant they hear in a word (e.g. L for 'liked'); later they might add a prominent end consonant (LT or LK), and later still a vowel (LAKT). These earliest attempts to represent *sounds* are gradually refined as *sight* (visual/graphic) letters are increasingly remembered from reading, for much reading is also proceeding day by day. Thus the daily influences of integrated listening-writing-reading serve to move the child rapidly towards standard spelling, e.g. 'liked' might develop in a single year through, say, L-LT-LKT-LAKT-LOKT-LIKT-LIKD-LIKED.

● In other words, natural classroom pressure moves *invention* towards correctness. While part of this pressure comes from the parallel reading program, it comes no less from the great amount of reading being done *while writing* — writing and reading continually reinforce each other.

● The teacher does not correct the child's first draft, but will write down a spelling if asked. (If a child's 'book' is 'published', the teacher will edit the spelling after explaining that this is what editors do to ensure that everyone can read books.)

● There is plenty of peer talk about story-line and spelling, and much reading of one another's writing.

● While spelling, a child often makes audible and sub-audible 'phonic' sounds, for at this transition stage the writing is more a *speech event* than a writing event.

● Accompanying the child's invention of spelling will be original invented marks which try to capture speech-emphasis, e.g. enlarged letters, bold letters, capitals, underlinings, multiple exclamation marks. These inventions too are accepted, even encouraged; later they will be voluntarily discarded as the child learns to rely on conventional forms.

— R. D. Walshe, *Every Child Can Write!*, P.E.T.A., 1981, p. 123.

3. Draft Writing   (*using 'invented spelling'*)

To learn to write is to learn an extraordinarily complex set of human behaviours. All authorities agree on that.[3] So great is writing's complexity that teachers can't *tell* children how to write; at best they can only explain or drill some formal aspects of writing. For the rest the children basically 'learn to write by writing', similar to the way they 'learned to talk by talking' in earlier years. So the conference approach strives to engage a young child's great language-learning potential in the enterprise of keenly and confidently 'writing' — and thus learning to write — about self-chosen interests.

The Key Principle: Leave Control with the Child

The key principle of the conference approach is: *leave the control (or responsibility or 'ownership') of the writing in the child's hands* — and this can be done from the first. It requires, as we have already seen, that topic-choice be left with the child. It also requires that we do not insist on a 'right way' or 'correctness', especially in the matter of spelling. Why? Because the children are beginners. They should not be compelled to get their writing 'right' or 'correct' from the start. Instead we teachers should have faith in their desire to learn, to progress towards what adults can do. Given scope, they will continually strive towards correctness, but they should not be expected to achieve it all at once.

If we demand instant correctness we push them into the inertia of sticking to the little they know — we make experiment and originality too risky. So we must encourage them to learn to write by writing copiously and fearlessly, each child spelling, punctuating and forming sentences to the best of his or her individual ability. And as we scrutinise 'in conference' a child's performance we must curb our adult urge to tell or to correct everything, instead limiting ourselves to offering help with perhaps only one manifest need. This is 'teaching skills in context' at a pace the child can handle.

The Advantages of Using 'Invented Spelling' When Drafting

The conference approach regards 'invented spelling' as the immensely valuable *natural* path a beginner can take in expressing thought confidently in writing before he or she knows how to spell. It ends the traditional domination of learning-to-spell over learning-to-write. Now, using 'invented spelling', the child pushes ahead with learning to write, unhindered by fear of incorrect spelling — indeed, the rate of progress attested by these 27 teachers is exciting! Yet spelling is not ignored. Far from it. As we shall see, the 'inventing' turns out to be a method at least as effective as the old list-copy-and-drill method.

---

[3] As Marlene Scardamalia says, 'Even a casual analysis makes it clear that the number of things that must be dealt with simultaneously in writing is stupendous: handwriting, spelling, punctuation, word choice, syntax, textual connections, purpose, organization, clarity, rhythm, euphony, the possible reactions of various possible readers, and so on. To pay conscious attention to all of these would overload the information-processing capacity of the most towering intellects.' — *cit.* R. D. Walshe, *Every Child Can Write!* P.E.T.A., 1981, p. 154.

Before hearing from the teachers, let me sum up the advantages of using 'invented spelling' at the draft writing stage of the writing process: *The main concern in 'teaching writing' is to encourage expression on paper of the child's flow of thought, and this is safeguarded by 'invented spelling' which asks the child to 'spell' words in the best way he or she knows, rather than be held up or avoid the use of some words because of the teacher's insistence on always spelling correctly.* After all, spelling is one facet only of the multifaceted set of behaviours we call writing and it should never have been allowed to dominate the others.

Having made this clear, we can also note that there *is* a place in the conference approach for correct spelling. That place is not the child's first draft. But when the child has worked on the draft and improved it so that the teacher agrees it deserves to be 'published', then either the teacher will arrange for it to be typed with conventional spelling or will scribe such spellings above the invented ones (not in red) so that the child can write out a polished final form.

● **'At First, I Found Invented Spelling Hard to Accept': Evelyn Collaro.** In the previous year I had strongly upheld correct spelling; every child had a personal dictionary in which I wrote the words they didn't know but needed for their stories. It came as a shock to these children, now

Evelyn Collaro comments, 'I found it interesting to note the rapid development of young children's spelling skills and to see how close their representations are to the desired words'.

my Year 2, to hear me say, 'Invent the spellings you aren't sure of. Don't come to me — just *have a go!*' But it was even harder for me to accept this new approach after my years with the 'correctness' method.

Moreover, at first their 'known' spelling seemed to decline, for I noticed *thait* for *that*, *thay* for *they*, etc. I feared that 'invented spelling' and 'rough drafts' were developing laziness. But perhaps these lapses were due to a change of focus — the children were concentrating on the meaning of their stories rather than on spelling. Soon I became aware of advances which more than compensated: not only did their skill in approximating to correct spellings develop rapidly, but they began to *use words they needed* where before they kept to words they could spell, and they rapidly developed confidence in attacking writing situations they were not familiar with.

My method? Consistency is the key. Ask the children to write their own thoughts and not be afraid of words they can't spell — invent the spelling, and help one another to do so. Remind them that this is for their first or rough draft and that any pieces chosen for publication will be corrected, as is done in the adult world. (I asked them to continue using their personal dictionaries, writing in for future reference some or all of the corrected words) . . . Really it is much the way we adults write our reports, assignments, applications — we first do a draft, often making spelling errors, then we polish and correct.

While inventing, the children are learning much. Jodie, for example, asked her friend Jason, 'How do you spell *instance?*' Jason sounded the first syllable 'in . . . st' and wrote *inst* on a piece of paper. Then he said, 'The last part sounds like *once* without the *w* sound.' Jodie thereupon added *nce* on the end. 'M-m-m, something's missing.' They looked carefully. 'It could be *a* or *u*,' said Jodie and she tried both *instunce* and *instance*. 'That's it,' she said and wrote *instance* into the story.

- **'With This Approach the Children Are Learning Far More':** **Joan Ham.** In previous years it was I who chose and taught the language I considered the children needed, exercises in phonics, sight vocabulary and word-building. This year my Kindergarten children are largely choosing their own language experiences. The result is keener interest, increased learning and a relatively integrated language program. In a sense, they have become the masters of their own learning; *they* dictate what they want to learn and this far exceeds what I ever 'dictated' to them.

As they have learned more about writing — they write eagerly using invented spelling — their interest has gone up and then in turn the reading helps their writing . . . and so we have progressed confidently.

They are now more interested than any kinders I have known in stories of all kinds — stories read to them, stories told to them and above all the stories 'written' by themselves. They discuss not only the content of stories but the language, the form, and the relevance of illustrations. For instance, when I *tell* them a story now, we discuss how it could be written in a book and the kinds of illustrations that might be used.

● **Explaining Invented Spelling in Year 1: Debbie Brownjohn.**
My Year 1 class had used 'Breakthrough to Literacy' as part of their
reading program in Kindergarten. I found that they relied too much on
'Breakthrough' words and produced stilted stories such as 'I can run to
mum' or 'I see dad run'. So when I asked them to write real stories and use
invented spelling they were reluctant to break away from writing stories in
which they could spell 'correctly'.

After several unsuccessful attempts to extend their stories beyond the
'Breakthrough' words, I decided to write a story on the chalkboard. When
I came to words that I pretended I couldn't spell, I asked them to help me
write the sounds so that we could read the words later.

They enjoyed this activity. It had a 'play' spirit to it. And it was *our
breakthrough* to uninhibited 'having a go' at spelling whatever words were
needed. After all, if the teacher did it this way, why shouldn't they?

● **Explaining Invented Spelling in Year 2: Robyn Platt.** My
Year 2 had been trained to believe that correct spelling was always required. They looked at me in disbelief when I said, 'In your first draft I'm
more interested in *what* you say than in correct spelling'.

Now, at the end of their year of writing, they are veterans of invented
spelling. They know that draft-copy stage is not correct-spelling time.

*Invented spelling gives children control over their own writing and allows for uninterrupted
flow of thoughts.*

'*Do you think* wrapped *is spelt like this, John?*' asks 7 year old Sharron.

They are convinced that words are *their* tools, that they can attempt to write *any* word they need, and that correct spelling can be looked up in reference books.

It is clear to them that they can polish their spelling just as they can polish all other aspects of their writing (meaning, sequence, liveliness, paragraphing, punctuation, etc.) in the conference, editing, final rewriting and proofreading stages of the writing process, all of which become necessary when a draft is considered worthy of further revision for 'publication'. Moreover, they know that some of their classmates have an inbuilt grasp of 'adult spelling' and are always ready to share this.

● **A 'Guess Book' Helps Invented Spelling.** (*Robyn Platt continues . . .*) We recommend that a small auxiliary notebook can be a great aid in encouraging invented spelling. Every child in my class has one. We call it the Guess Book.

When a child feels the need to think out the spelling of a word before writing it into a story, the Guess Book is the place to test possible spellings — perhaps assisted by discussion with a classmate or the teacher. It may be used at the draft-writing stage but I find it is used more often at the revision/editing stage when work on a word doesn't stop the flow of story-making. Of course, beyond the Guess Book is the dictionary, but it will be most effectively resorted to if a close approximation to the spelling of the word has been achieved.

Two of my children are most regular in their use of the Guess Book. Emma, with a talent for spelling, tries out several versions of a word and then always seems to pick the correct one. Renee, younger and much less assured, also writes several versions but is then likely to call for the assistance of teacher or peer. Either way the Book helps them by providing a means of trying out sounds and letter-combinations on paper before making a decision.

**How Invented Spelling
Enabled 5 Year Old Greg
to Write a Story
He Could Not Otherwise Have Written**

For several months Greg was satisfied to draw his stories. Then one day be began to add a few letters . . . within three weeks he had taken off into writing. Here is a story that took him three writing sessions:

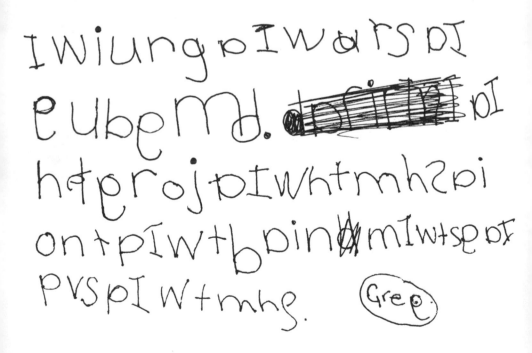

Translated, it reads:

I   w   i   u   rg   a   I   w   a   rs   a   I
I was in a rocket and I won the race and I

g   u   b   g   md.   ~~darirInI~~ a   I
got a big gold medal.   and I

 h   tg   r   o   j   a   I   w   h   t   m   hs   a   i
had to get lots of drinks and I went home to my house and it

 o   n   t   a   I w   t   b   a   i   n   d̸   m   I w
was night time and I went to bed and it was day morning. I went

t   sg   a   I p   vs   a   I w   t   m   hs.
to school and I played with friends and I went to my house.

Tuesday Morning: Greg drew a picture and had begun to write its story when recess interrupted.

Tuesday Afternoon: Given free choice after finishing a craft activity, he returned to his story. I could see him sounding out words, sounding, writing, reading-back and then writing some more. At one point he crossed out a part and said, 'That bit's wrong'. Later he again left the writing unfinished.

Wednesday Morning: He took it up again, commenting that it was going to be a very long story. He re-read what he had written, continued writing for some time, and at last said, 'Finished!'

In conference with me, he began to read it but stopped after 'house'. 'Could it be *and I*?' I asked. 'No,' he replied firmly, pointing to the *i*, 'that sound says *i* not *I*—m-m-m, it says *and it*.' He crossed out *d* for *day* before *morning*, saying 'I don't need that'. But when I suggested he needed a *with* (towards the end) he pointed to the *v* in *friends* and wouldn't be budged.

Though he mainly writes only initial sounds at this stage, Greg is showing remarkable control over his writing. *He* is doing the learning and at an incredible speed. Without invented spelling he could not have written this piece. It is genuine writing, put aside and taken up several times while remaining fully under the child's control. Even scribing could not have achieved this result, because then the pen would have been in the teacher's hand, the piece would probably have had to be done at a single session, and the teacher would have been sorely tempted to 'help' in small ways. (*Lurline Grime*)

Seven old year Belinda talks to herself as she revises the first draft of her story, 'The Three Brown Bears.'

4. Preparing for Publication

To 'revise' or 'edit' is an important part of the writing process, but it is not something young writers will do spontaneously. They tend to *write* as they *speak*, not feeling any need to revise either utterance. So the teacher has to introduce them to revising, but must do so gently and patiently.

This, indeed, is why I am using the heading 'Preparing for Publication' rather than 'Revision' or 'Editing'—as a reminder, not to teach revision/ editing to the young as a set of exercises, but rather to *present it as a necessary act of polishing those special pieces of our writing which we hope will be published.*[1]

---

[1] Of course the teacher can try a 'counsel of perfection': encourage children to self-edit *every* draft, both as a matter of pride and as good self-discipline. Editing, in its full meaning, is a writer's 'unlimited striving to improve both the surface and the depths of a draft' (R. D. Walshe, *Every Child Can Write!*, P.E.T.A., Sydney, 1981, p. 40. This book contains an extensive study of the writing process including detailed treatment of 'Revising').

Influencing Children to Value Editing

(1) Point out that all adult published writing is edited.
(2) Regularly examine commercially produced books to notice that every one is a polished production.
(3) Regularly discuss 'what readers expect' of a writer (e.g. clear ideas, in good sequence, correct spelling, good punctuation).
(4) Regularly specify the potential readers of a class-produced book: classmates, children in other classes, parents, teachers.
(5) Explain that publication is 'competitive' in the sense that not everything one writes but only one's very best work — work with reader appeal — can be published.
(6) Above all, notice and applaud every good example of classroom published work, instancing the features that make it appealing.

The very young ('egocentric') writer is not at first interested in editing his or her writing. Once this writing has been shown to the teacher, the writer's inclination is to leave it and move to something new. But with time and a growing awareness that readers can be critical, especially peer readers, the idea of editing takes hold.

Preparing for Publication in a Conference

● **Before a major editing conference:** ask the child to (1) re-read and re-work the piece, checking to see that the 'Things I Can Do' in the Writing Folder have all been done; (2) read the piece to a 'writing partner' for an opinion; (3) (for older children) share the piece with a group or the whole class for varied responses.

● **During the editing conference:**
.. leave 'control', and the pencil, in the child's hand;
.. if you need to demonstrate something, write it on a separate piece of paper and the child may then copy this;
.. if the child cannot grasp a point, call on a few classmates for suggestions (we found that quite young writers, 6 year olds, will more readily listen to suggestions from peers than from the teacher);
.. when questioning has clarified a story-line and the child is satisfied with the piece, the teacher may discern and discuss a 'teaching point' that can advance the child's understanding (this is a very different approach from feeling that everything has to be 'corrected' by the teacher);
.. if the invented spelling can't be read without the child's assistance, the teacher can write the story at the bottom of the page, explaining that this is for the typist (it is not then seen as 'marking' or 'correcting');
.. discuss how much of the story should go on each page when the book is published;
.. if the child, not a typist, is going to write out the final published version then the teacher will similarly supply conventional spelling and punctuation, explaining to the child that 'readers will expect it';
.. the teacher is, finally, the 'chief executive' of the class's 'publishing firm' and as such must uphold a standard of quality, asking for the best that the writers are known to be capable of (e.g. compare a current piece with a superior previous publication by the writer); and writing not

good enough for publication must reluctantly be rejected if the writer is unwilling to revise it in the light of teacher and peer suggestions;

.. value especially your *questioning skill*, sensing when to press this young thinker and when to refrain from causing feelings of frustration; allow sufficient 'wait time' (up to 8 seconds) before the next question; above all, avoid talking too much.

When writing partners work together they help to lift the quality of each other's writing.

CHAPTER 6

Publishing the Writing

The essence of 'publication' is not just *producing* a 'book'; it is getting the writing to real readers—*getting it read*. Writers need to think hard about their intended readers, about what will interest them, and about a form of publication that will attract them.

Why Jason Likes to Publish His Writing

'I like writing this way because I have something I can be proud of,' says 7 year old Jason, showing me the latest of his several typewritten books.

'When I've finished a good story, the typist types it and I've got a book the other kids want to read. They like reading my books and that makes me feel real proud.

'It's different with the stories that just stay in my Writing Folder. No one reads them. But the ones that will get published, I don't mind fixing up the spelling and fullstops and all that stuff because then the typist can understand it, and when I get it back it looks real great.'

'I like writing this way because I have something I can be proud of,' says 7 year old Jason.

The essence of 'publication' is not just producing a 'book'. It is getting the writing to real readers—getting it read! Robyn Platt has found that interest and ability in reading in her Year 2 class has been stimulated through writing.

How the Teachers Handled Publishing

Knowing how stimulating publishing is to young authors like Jason, the 27 teachers in the project all made some arrangement for publishing their children's books.

- *One in Four.* Children need to realise that only their best writing deserves to be published. The 'best of four or five pieces' was the general rule the teachers established, with the child having the say about what was best. But the rule was flexible in allowing, say, for two consecutive stories being 'best' while the ensuing five or six might be relatively flat.
- *Benign Censorship.* While the child makes the choice, the teacher retains a right to turn down language or content that is offensive or hurtful.
- *Attractive Product.* The finished product must appeal widely—must bid for readers on a 'competitive market'. The teachers ensured that 'mechanics' of spelling, punctuation and grammar met conventional expectations. (Mild grammatical variance was tolerated for these small children, but 'brung' was edited to 'brought', 'I are' to 'I am', and so on.) The stories were mostly bound in wallpaper-offcuts, light cardboard or heavy coloured paper.

● *Typed or Handwritten.* In several classes mothers volunteered to type the stories, at school or at home. In others some teachers did the typing, while some preferred to write (print) them by hand. Occasionally, but increasingly in Year 2, some children chose to handwrite the stories for themselves (the choice was entirely theirs).

● *A 'Publishing Company'.* The largest school in the Project, Sylvania Heights, decided to set up its own publishing company, here described by its Infants Mistress, Barbara Fiala . . .

A Publishing Company in the Infants Department

Our school possesses a large-print typewriter which we felt would be ideal for presenting the children's published books. It was! Everyone looked forward to the miracle of seeing an edited 'draft' turned into attractive print.

But, alas, the volume of work from twelve classes swamped our slender typing resources. In panic we sent a letter to all our parents explaining what we were doing and requesting help with typing, either by typing at school or at home. More parents offered to do so at home than at school, so we allocated the Year 2 typing to the home typists and assigned our large-print machine to the Kindergarten and Year 1 children. A typing roster was duplicated and sent to parents and staff.

Daily, every teacher handed in a class folder of the children's writings which were sorted and distributed for typing. When the typing was done, the teachers' aide stapled it into serviceable covers which carried the title, author's name and date. The books together with the authors' returned 'manuscripts' then went to the class for handing to the proud authors, who promptly shared them with classmates. This whole publishing process usually took no more than two days.

Our splendid parent helpers said they enjoyed the work and gained insight into the children and an understanding of this fascinating new way of teaching writing. Some typical comments from them:

'The range of topics is amazing!'
'Just listen to this child's imagination . . .'
'I didn't know they had it in them!'
'I typed 24 pages for one story!'

Self-reliance Born

Five year old Kate wanted the spelling of *walk* for her story. After several minutes searching for it on the 'Breakthrough' stand, she returned to her table muttering, 'Can't find it. I'll just have to work it out for myself.'

Chapter 7

Programming and Evaluation

- 'How do you program this writing approach?'
- 'How do you evaluate the children's writing?'

I was frequently asked these questions by teachers who visited the three Project schools. As the year progressed my answer became briefer and clearer till it went something like this:

> 'We neither program nor evaluate our writing in the old way. The old ("modified traditional") way of *programming* commonly demanded a 5-weekly prescription of teacher-devised topics (and sometimes methods), while the old way of *evaluating* commonly meant correcting a child's first draft and assigning it a mark, stamp, 'Good' or whatever. Those practices suited a regimen of whole-class instruction which cast the learners in a passive-receptive role awaiting "input" from the teacher; but they are practices quite unsuited to the individualised learning of the conference approach.'

This was of course only the negative side of my answer. I wanted to stress that the new approach needed a new conception of both programming and evaluation. I then went on to explain, first, that this approach greatly simplifies programming, and, second, that it enables the teacher to amass an effective evaluation record, not by time-consuming testing, but by procedures which are incidental to every day's teaching.

1. Simplified Programming

The essential program can be expressed in one sentence and it remains valid for all through the year: *In the daily writing period, each child in my class will work individually, writing on his or her self-chosen topic within the framework of the process-conference approach.*

Obviously no teacher can plan an old-style, general *class writing program* when the children are working individually, each choosing a topic, each retaining control (or 'ownership') at all stages of the writing, and each progressing at his or her level. What now in fact happens is that, every day, each child sets his or her own writing program.

If more than a single-sentence teaching program is asked for by anyone, then the teacher can provide an outline of how-writing-happens-in-my-class, a synopsis of the process-conference approach (e.g. based on the 'Proposal' which launched the St. George Project). Here is such an outline devised by Robyn Platt:

> **'The Program of the Conference Approach.** This is a well-researched program for individualising the learning of written expression. Its key principle is that each writer keeps control (or "ownership") of the writing at all stages. The children write every day for (say) half an hour on topics of their own choosing. For beginning writers, drawing and "invented spelling" are considered to be integral

parts of the writing process. The children write a draft in an unconstrained manner which allows them to concentrate on content; they are then encouraged to revise and polish both the content and the formal features, not hesitating to call on peer assistance as they do so. A proportion of their best work is "published"; that is, it is conveyed to readers in an attractive form, often as class-made "books" which become an important reading resource in the class library.

'The teacher assists chiefly by organising this "writing classroom" and by being available for "conferences", one-to-one discussions between teacher and writer. Several conferences normally take place during a "process of writing", which stretches from topic-selection through drafting to final editing for publication. Each child builds up a Folder of writings which, together with his or her published books, is a record that can be shown to parents and next year's teacher.'

(This outline could surely be varied to take in additional procedures specially valued by any teacher.)

'Records Become the Program'. Robyn Platt points out that: 'Every conference is a teaching time, but the teacher cannot predict (i.e. program) the teaching that needs to be done until the child presents his or her writing. Then two teaching responses become possible: first, the teacher can bring to bear on the writing her general insight into this child's needs, an insight deepened by frequent individual conferencing; second, the teacher can sharpen her judgment of how-to-help by glancing at her records of the child's strengths and weaknesses. By either or both of these paths the teacher will arrive at a decision on the "teaching point" which will best meet the child's current need. This means, if you think about it, that the teaching "program" is really the *records* accumulated in the teacher's mind and on paper, for they alone are reliable guides to an individual child's needs.' (Later we will see what such written records can be. —*J. T.*)

The Wider Language Program. Lurline Grime has found that the conference approach to writing has led her into integrating other aspects of her language program with writing. For example, she collects *and writes down* examples of baby speech, lazy speech, and mispronunciations; then she uses rhymes and jingles which help to overcome these deficiencies. Thus the Speech Program is improved by the precision which writing brings.

Even more, the Reading Program merges with the Writing Program, each reinforcing the other. Books read to, or read by, the children obviously influence *what* and *how* they write. So the teachers in the Project became more careful than ever before in their choice of books to read and to make available to the children. They programmed the use of a variety of kinds of books. All agreed that the 'books' published by the children themselves deserve as much prominence in the classroom and as much promotion as the bought books.

As to the subject areas beyond language itself, many teachers realised they could harness the children's new love of writing to the work in those areas. They realised at the same time that such writing should follow the main principles of the conference approach; in particular a high level of choice of topic needs to be left with each child and 'conference conditions' of writing need to be observed. Different subject areas demand different writing modes, e.g. letters, lists in Science. (Carolyn Bowman tells how she did this in Social Studies, see p. 46.)

2. Evaluation Records

The mistresses of the three schools involved in the Project agreed that evaluation should be kept simple for the teachers and helpful for the learners. Too often in the past, they had seen evaluation become either a mystery or a monster: a mystery insofar as teachers have acted in blind faith that a child's total performance in the complex craft of writing could be evaluated by testing-and-numerical-marking (only a few surface features of writing can in fact be so tested); a monster insofar as teachers have been diverted from fostering a willingness to write as they piled up a weight of 'evaluation for evaluation sake' — or a principal's sake or parent's sake.

There are four shareholders in the enterprise of evaluation — child, teacher, principal, parent. How can the interests of all of them be satisfied?

The Project schools decided not to impose a system of evaluation on the teachers but to treat the problem experimentally and see what the teachers discovered by trial-and-error. Here is the picture that I believe has emerged.

● **Part of Every Day's Teaching.** Put simply, to evaluate is to 'look at how things are going' and 'make a judgment about how to help things forward'. In the conference approach this looking and judging is individualised because each child works at his or her own level. (Little of value would be revealed by whole-class testing and rank-ordering of results.) The teachers all felt that the daily writing, the frequent conferencing and the periodic publication of every child's best work all helped to give a teacher an intimate understanding of the child's strengths, needs and rate of progress. The following findings seem broadly to be agreed on:
(a) the most significant evaluation record is in the teacher's head, and while this can be termed 'impressionistic' and 'subjective', there is no reason to use these terms disparagingly;
(b) all the teachers supplemented their subjective record with a *record book* of some kind, an anecdotal record or 'profile' of day-by-day jotted observations;
(c) at various times throughout the year teachers went through each child's Writing Folder in an attempt to notice patterns emerging over time, not observed during classroom work;
(d) all the teachers saw the Writing Folder as an evaluation resource to which they could refer if required to discuss a child's progress (they saw to it that this Folder included a page headed 'Things I Have Learned', being the child's self-evaluation);
(e) some teachers kept, in a special file for each child, samplings from each term's best writings;

The conference helps to give a teacher an intimate understanding of the child's strengths, needs and rate of progress. Linda Mein mentally notes such understandings as she listens attentively to 5 year old Joanna read her 'invented spelling'.

(f) early in the year some teachers felt a need for 'skills checklists' in the belief that these would enable them to help the children, but I think all of these were abandoned as the children's progress and the wide range of the class's abilities made every list too restrictive.

In sum, the teachers felt they knew their children better than ever before; the mistresses felt the teachers' written records and work samples were more than adequate; and the parents, as we shall now see, felt that they were better informed about their children's progress than they expected to be.

Communication with Parents

From the start the three schools saw the importance of keeping parents briefed on this new approach. An initial explanatory letter was sent to them and they were invited periodically to meetings which answered questions and demonstrated the progress by showing work samples. The parents were asked to support the schools at home and, if possible to help at school (as 'parent aides'). Each of the schools communicated somewhat differently with the parents.

● **Grays Point.** As well as an initial meeting, grade meetings, and several letters on the conference approach, parents could inspect a 'Progress Book' which was sent to them in the 6th and 13th weeks of each term. It showed their child's writing of one week in all subject areas; and when a 'draft' copy and a 'polished' copy had been done, both were included. An end-of-year report summed up the child's progress as a writer.

● **Hurstville South.** Strong efforts were made to reach all parents and particularly those whose mother tongue is not English. A meeting early in the year was very successful; later the parents were continually invited to inspect what was happening; on one occasion an explanatory letter was sent out in Arabic. The teachers sent home an 'Evaluation Folder' containing two examples of a draft together with its polished copy, the first written at the beginning of term, the other at the end; and specific comments were added. An end-of-year report discussed how far the child had come, whether he or she was enjoying writing, the variety of stories being produced, and skills that were now being confidently used. The teachers intend to meet early next year to consider ways of improving still further their contacts with the parents.

● **Sylvania Heights.** As well as its letters and meetings, this school too has used a 'Progress Book'. Sent home in June and November it is a folder into which is stapled the child's best, polished draft and the published book

Seven year old Darren shares his famous published story, '20,000 Leagues under the Pie', with his group.

made from that draft. A checklist is included which can be quickly filled out by the teacher to help track the child's progress.

Has any teacher ever proclaimed that a scheme of evaluation is totally satisfactory? Our Project teachers would not wish to do so. However, keeping a teacher's record, keeping work samples, helping children to keep their own records, and communicating frequently with the parents—these accomplishments are seen as a firm base on which we can build further next year.

Example of a letter to parents . . .

Dear Parent

Your child has made progress under our new WRITING PROGRAM and I am pleased to report this progress below. But first let me remind you of some features of our approach.

We value writing because we know that, with reading, it is the key to success in nearly all later learning. So we give writing more than average time, and we teach it in specially stimulating conditions.

Everyone learns language best by using it in real-life situations. In that way we all learned painlessly to talk, and our Program is similarly teaching your child to write—by writing about real interests. In fact we are sure this is the best way to teach not only the correct use of language but also what is even more important: how to express original thoughts.

Our Program encourages your child to choose interesting topics freely, to write abundantly, to be original, to discuss problems whenever 'blocks' arise, and to use words boldly, even words which cannot yet be spelt correctly but can be attempted phonetically (technically termed 'invented spelling'). Avoiding over-correction, which undermines confidence, we correct the proportion of your child's writing which can at that stage be understood; but we do fully 'edit' (or correct) the pieces which are rewritten and honoured by 'publication as a book', which your child illustrates for inclusion in the classroom library.

If, as well as all this writing at school, your child wishes to write at home, please be encouraging—see that the writing is a pleasure, praise it, and date it so that you have a record of your child's progress. Our guiding principle: *Writing alway progresses when children write with interest and adults show interest in what they have written.*

[Report on child follows . . .]

CHAPTER 8

'Not Only Writing Improves . . .'

Before the project had run its first term, several teachers remarked, 'You know, it's not only their writing that's improving . . .'
- 'My kids are reading better than any Year 1 I've taught.' (*J.B.*)
- 'Peter has stopped being a behaviour problem.' (*R.P.*)
- 'They're trying new things in all lessons, especially art.' (*J.A.*)
- 'There's a general growth of confidence about learning.' (*W.G.*)

Such comments have snowballed since.

When I asked the teachers why so many notable by-products of this writing approach had surfaced, they offered a variety of reasons:
.. The 'conference approach' puts the child in a classroom situation which makes an active learning role seem natural;
.. an active role flows from the high degree of responsibility (initiative) given to the child in choosing subject-matter, setting the learning-rate, and seeing the task through;
.. readily accepting these responsibilities, the child is more inclined to perform at peak than in teacher-imposed conditions;
.. carrying out self-chosen, interesting tasks the child is largely self-motivated and typically becomes busy in the work;
.. there is adequate time for practising the whole process of writing *and* its associated talking, reading, research, reflection;
.. self-selected goals are regularly achieved and this not only brings satisfaction but builds self-confidence;
.. the teacher is always at hand to assist, encourage, praise (fear of criticism, rebuff or failure is absent);
.. all the children receive more *individual* attention from the teacher and other adults than in previous conditions.

There is only room to present a small selection of 'case studies' which will give the reader an insight into the way this writing approach produces improvements in other learning areas. (Incidentally, I value the strong opinion of Marie Mann and Jim Findlay, experienced Resource Teachers at the two largest schools, that this is by far the best approach to 'remedial' education known to them.) Five teachers have supplied these case studies.

(1) From Non-reader to Reader through Writing

Fred, age 8, came into my 'remedial' Year 2 class because he showed neither interest nor ability in reading. Yet he was a fine artist. His pictures could tell a 'story' in detail and they revealed that he had an outstanding general knowledge. He spent our 'writing time' drawing but would not write about his pictures.

Because the conference approach stresses a relationship between drawing and writing, Fred soon felt that his drawings were part of the classroom's writing interests. Teacher and classmates kept asking him to *explain* more about his drawings. In particular his confidence was boosted

Seven year old Fred is a keen illustrator who at first refused to write, but through the patience and supportive environment offered by Liz Marshall, he has begun to write and read.

as children asked for his help in illustrating their stories. He began to realise that he had to *read* the words of their stories or they would get upset: 'You've drawn a tank when—look!—what I wrote is enemy land cruisers,' complained Michael. He also realised that writing underneath a drawing could prevent misinterpretations.

He began to write captions to his drawings. Now he was at last writing and reading for strongly practical purposes. In a very short time his written stories became as detailed as his drawings, his spelling skills developed rapidly, and he was reading for enjoyment and to find information for further stories . . . Fred is now a confident boy and no one would dream of calling him a 'remedial' learner. (*Liz Marshall*)

(2) From 'Behaviour Problem' to Active Learner

Gordon, age 7, had been a problem from his first day in Kindergarten. He learnt little, scarcely spoke, avoided reading, and now here he was, staring blankly at the page when I asked him to write. His only interest was in poking and punching other children. He was in my Year 2 class only because his parents had objected to a strong recommendation that he should repeat Year 1.

I talked to him several times in the first week before he took up a suggestion that he could use *any* writing implement and do *anything* on the page. Choosing the brightest textas he drew ghosts, bats, castles and witches, folding and turning a large sheet as he did so. Asked to explain the pictures, he grunted, 'It's bats, ghosts.' I asked if he'd like to write about them. 'Can't,' he replied, obviously wanting to escape to his sport of poking and punching. So I took a desperate plunge: 'Would you like me to write for you?' At his direction I began to label bats, ghosts, witches . . .

Next day we talked some more and he shyly asked me to write, 'This is a witch. She is in her castle with her cat.' For the next few days he drew almost identical pictures until to my surprise he wrote

The wich is c   at to t   in fogs.
The witch is going to turn people into frogs.

Next day he drew a picture of ghosts, followed by a one-sentence story which he asked me to caption as 'My Scarey House'. I read this to the class and several children took up the topic 'My Scarey House'. This was prestige! (He knew that the other children had had a poor opinion of him.) Suddenly he was off—talking, making rocket ship noises, suggesting stories. He became sought after as a writing partner. Within two weeks he was doing things he had never done in his previous two school years. Working busily he stopped poking and punching.

At first he preferred working with others; later he published many good stories alone. His reading improved. He also reads orally with expression.

'To tell the truth, I never thought Gordon would ever learn to read—but now, through writing his own stories, he is reading and enjoying it,' says Wendy Goebel.

At the kindergarten stage, Margaret Newton finds writing an ideal opportunity to relate one-to-one to each child and build up that special rapport.

And his abilities have extended to other subjects. I now have every confidence that, with a little help at some points, he will cope with next year's primary school work. (*Wendy Goebel*)

(3) From Silence and Inactivity to Talking and Writing

Robert at 5 years old was physically smaller, less mature and less fluent orally than many 3 year olds. In class he played by himself, took no interest in what others were doing, rarely communicated with anyone, lived in a world of his own.

The conference approach, I was finding, is an ideal opportunity to work individually with every child — and I sensed that Robert needed more of my time and encouragement than most. Day after day I spent a few minutes with him, slowly building up his trust in me.

He began to speak a little more loudly, to repeat a question, to echo new words . . . I felt like celebrating when he first volunteered something — though I didn't let on that I hadn't understood a word! Each day he would do a drawing and we would talk a little more about this work. My cautious questions would coax a few more words from him. At length we could hold quite a conversation together. His pronunciations and sentence structures were often poor and difficult to understand and I would speak some of them back for him to repeat.

At present my emphasis is on his oral expression *but it is in the writing time that we are achieving most success in this area.* Moreover he *is* now 'writing', though only strings of letters under drawings, such as

I rolEaooAl

He read this to me as, 'I going in truck'. I wrote up his 'baby speech' in a grammatical sentence and with additions it has become a published book, *Trucks*, which he proudly 'reads', sometimes looking to me for help. I will say, 'I'm going in the truck', and though he usually translates in baby speech ('I going . . .'), I know he will soon follow my model.

Many of my children are well on the way to reading and writing success; they will work alone for long periods and talk purposefully with their peers. But less mature children like Robert need a trusted adult with them for at least a few minutes every day in the writing time. It is the only way to make sure of their progress. (*Margaret Newton*)

Margaret Cooper displays class theme reference words in a variety of ways in her classroom.

(4) From a Refusal-to-Write to a Willingness

Six year old David began to write but then stopped. In February-March of Year 1 he had drawn pictures and attempted stories to go with them, for example

I m y te he b B V

(*His reading:* 'My dad went to the beach.')

But in April he seemingly 'regressed' to pictures only. This may have been connected with my decision in that month to wean the class from 'Breakthrough to Literacy' because I felt it was cultivating stiff, stereotyped language. I urged the children to use their own words and boldly invent the spelling. His classmates quickly found their new 'wings' and leapt ahead in writing ability. Not so David. In conference he would *tell* me about his drawing, he was happy for me to be his scribe, but he refused to write himself.

I decided to give him time. For three months he went on drawing or watching other children writing. In July his mother mentioned that he could not be encouraged to write at home either. It was then that I decided I must find those 'wings' for him. I told him firmly that he was going to *write* a story to accompany one of his picture sequences.

'I can't do it!' he protested. So I asked him what happened in the first drawing *then sat with him while he painstakingly wrote every word.* It was an unusually long conference and sometimes tearful. I praised each word as he laboriously spelt it but declined to spell a single one for him. I found that he *could* write! In fact, comparison of this July writing with his last writing (February) revealed surprising progress. During his months of no writing he had obviously been influenced by our 'writing classroom'; after all, he had been drawing, listening to children sounding out invented spellings, reading their work, and no doubt doing some written composing *in his head.* His first sentence was: *This is a funy boat.* He had acquired spacing, phonic skills, spelling skills. In this single conference, as the tearfulness passed, he too found that he could write—and he was clearly proud.

David had felt so insecure about his ability that he shied away from trying. I think he is one of a very few children who need gentle coercion at a crisis stage in learning to write. Once secure as to his ability, no further problems of this kind arose. His general confidence expanded . . . I wonder if other teachers will agree with my handling of David's 'block'? (*Margaret Cooper*)

(5) From Hesitation to Confident English—an E.S.L. Child[1]

This 'conference approach' helps the E.S.L. children to learn to write just as much as it does the English-speaking children, but I believe it helps them even more in other areas. At my school, Hurstville South, with its large proportion of E.S.L. children, I have observed it improving their reading, their behaviour, and their self-esteem and confidence.

---

[1] This, for the uninitiated, is a learner who is using English as a second language.

Robyn Legge finds that the writing time is a part of the day when she and Mouemin work cooperatively.

Take the case of Mouemin, a Lebanese boy in my Year 1 class of 34 children. At the beginning of the year his English was poor and he seemed to have more trouble learning it than most Lebanese children. His frustration often showed in disruptive behaviour.

Lacking verbs, he could only give me labels for his story-drawings. Thus he knew the word 'house' and brought me a drawing of many types of houses with that single word underneath. Questioning him I found that this was in fact a story about the homes of all his relatives. I helped him with English words he didn't know, such as 'uncle', 'cousin', and 'grandfather', and also with sentence structures, writing these under the appropriate pictures. Then he read back to me with some prompting.

When this piece was published for Mouemin he was so proud of it he would read it to anyone who would listen. In doing so he constantly practised the English structures that he currently needed. His next piece was almost a rewrite of that story but he wrote it on his own and could read it without hesitation. He slowly moved from stories of houses and cousins to a wider world. His last piece for the year was a detailed five-page story of a trip to Warragamba Dam. He has to interpret some of his invented spelling to me but I am thrilled by the rapid English language development that is taking place. And there is no more disruptive behaviour. (*Robyn Legge*)

Robyn makes the following answer to my question (J.T.):

How Do You Think Teachers Can Best Help E.S.L. Children to Write by the Conference Approach?

● *First, be patient.* I had to keep reminding myself not to expect too much too soon. Moreover it took me two terms to learn 'their language'—I mean their attempts to communicate in English. At first, progress seems non-existent but now, over a period, I see that progress has certainly occurred.

● *Second, provide practice.* Any skill needs regular practice. My Lebanese children, for example, especially needed practice in writing in a script and direction different from the script and direction of their culture—and needed to be able to do so without fear of rebuke for 'getting it wrong'.

● *Third, accept all efforts.* Not only encourage them to 'have a go' but be prepared to accept all honest efforts even though these (temporarily) include English words and structures that are 'incorrect'. Like 'invented spelling' this is a transitional strategy: many influences are working on the child to correct his or her writing over time—but only if the child *does* write, copiously and with interest and confidence.

● *Fourth, tap into the children's experience.* Everyone agrees that children write best about their own freely chosen experiences, but E.S.L. children are often reluctant to write in class about home experiences however rich. Perhaps this is because these experiences have, as it were, happened in the mother tongue and call for difficult translation; or it could be a reluctance to reveal culturally different happenings in an

While Sister Kathleen talks with Kate, Simone checks a word from the word bank, and James and Chris work on their stories.

Australian classroom. Whatever the reason, we can help out by providing plenty of vivid *school experiences*, shared by all the class—subjects and language common to every child. At the same time I ask my whole class to study aspects of the culture of our larger E.S.L. groups—for example a subject dear to our Lebanese children, the Ramadan festival—so that E.S.L. children can take the lead, speaking up and writing about their culture.

• *Finally, be open to other cultures.* The Ramadan study proved to be quite a breakthrough! It showed how much teachers need to adjust to '*multi*' cultural thinking. A multicultural consultant can of course help greatly. We are building up resource materials on the cultures of our E.S.L. children. We want these children to feel uninhibited about bringing their homes to school just as English-speaking children do—and take the school home so as to give parents a better idea of what the school is trying to do.

'Guess what, Sister Kath-a-leen? I wrote 33 words!'

Kate was 'an uncooperative child'. Unlike most of the other 5 year olds she lacked the confidence to begin drawing and writing early in the year. A June entry in my logbook, 'Slowly breaking through', reminds me that not till then did I see small signs of initiative which I hoped might lead to confidence.

Later in June she began a conference by actually saying she would like to draw something; and during July she attempted to write for the first time. Since then her confidence in herself and in others has developed rapidly.

Kate has been fortunate in having supportive, attentive teaching in a vibrant classroom, part of which has been daily conferences about drawing/writing. By the end of the year she had blossomed into a competent writer who enjoys learning.

Why her early uncooperative attitude? An only child, she was shattered by the death of her beloved Grandfather in the year before she came to school. Significantly she has now found she can *write* about her 'Pop':

KATE

I like My pop. My pop is in the hsptl   He is in hFN Nh.
I like my pop to cmBc. KATE like hR pop. [*And, captioning a drawing:*] KATE is FsiTn hR pop.   Im pop.[1]

Kate showed this to me with mingled pride and delight: 'Guess what? You don't know what I wrote! I bet you can't read it, Sister Kath-a-leen. I wrote thirty-three words!'

Sister Kathleen Hill

(Sister Kathleen is investigating the writing process in 5 year olds at St. Bernard's Primary School, East Coburg, Victoria. She writes: 'I think I have enough material to compile my own book!'—*J. T.*)

[1] KATE/I like my pop. My pop is in the hospital. He is in heaven now. I like my pop to come back. Kate likes her pop./Kate is visiting her pop./I'm pop.

Part 2: The Conference Approach in the Primary Years 3-6

Introduction

No one could quarrel with the view that every teacher, about to take a new class, should ask, *'How were the children taught to write last year?'*.

Unfortunately that question hasn't always been asked. But the need to ask it has become imperative now that the 'conference approach' is making rapid headway across Australia.

For years to come, we will have a mixed scene. There will be K-2 teachers saying, 'We worry about sending our confident young writers on to a primary school that knows nothing of the conference approach'. And there will be Years 3-6 teachers who *have* taken up the approach and who wish that previous teachers of their latest class had tried it.

In such a time of change we must safeguard the children from 'culture shock', in this case neither thrusting them insensitively from 'new' back to 'old' nor rushing them from 'old' to 'new' without preparation. Accordingly:

● We ask every primary teacher to study the K-2 story in the foregoing pages. *Don't treat it as kids' stuff!* What these 5-8 year olds have learned, while human potential for language-acquisition was at its height, will profoundly influence their performance throughout the primary school years.

● In fact this conference approach, with its scrupulous respect for 'process', has inducted each of the children into self-discovery of an effective individual way of writing ('the child's unique process') which will probably remain his or her true 'basics of writing' for life. Anything added in the primary or secondary years will have to be built on that K -2 base.[1]

IN PART 2, then, let us follow exactly the chapter heads of Part 1, for the procedures of Years 3-6 will not differ in principle from the procedures detailed for K-2 and so there is no need to repeat them. This means that the chapters of Part 2 can be kept brief. They have been put together from reports sent to P.E.T.A. rather arbitrarily from various parts of Australia. They are obviously only a fraction of what might have been gathered if there had been time, opportunity and the resources to publish a larger book.

---

[1] This point about the true 'basics of writing' is fundamental to understanding the development of writing ability across the K-12 range. The 'process-conference approach', as reported in these pages, has given the K-2 children a grounding in the discovery and control of individual writing process. The confidence thus inspired will enable them as they advance through Years 3-12 to face every kind of writing problem, whether concerned with content, style, mode, or a variety of purposes and readers.

CHAPTER 1

Launching the Conference Approach

How might the conference approach be launched — or selectively trialled — in a primary school?

Begin by discussing the approach with your Executive Staff. Of course, before there is any launching, one or more teachers need to be well briefed. This can be achieved fairly quickly by studying this book; better still, by also referring to the books recommended on page 14.

A lighter briefing of the rest of the staff can immediately be achieved by handing around copies of the *Proposal* which launched the St. George Project (p. 10). (There is no need to ask P.E.T.A. for copyright permission, or St. George Regional Office, or the author. — *J.T.*) You can modify the *Proposal* to suit local needs, e.g. you might wish to allow more time for writing than the suggested half hour daily.

- *Julia Smith, Newbridge Hts P.S., after trying the approach in 1981:*
  'I think it is up to three or four of our teachers to spread the word throughout the school — to encourage others to dispense with outdated methods, to join the new wave of writers!'

- *Tony Moore, Liverpool Region (NSW), Language Consultant:*
  'We launched a conference-approach Writing Project in four K-6 schools with different socio-economic intakes, involving at first only two teachers from each school. They attended an in-service and were asked to adapt the ideas to their classrooms. Another consultant and I visited them periodically but we found ourselves conferencing with the children rather than advising the teachers, who swiftly grasped the approach. Since then two more teachers from each school have joined the project and there will be further expansion next year.'

- *Cathy Hickson, Leppington Primary School:*
  'How could such an obvious method of teaching writing remain undiscovered for so long? It is so unified and complete and brings me such satisfaction!'

'At Last the Children Are Really Writing!'

'I now realise that what we have been calling "Writing" has mostly been a series of imposed exercises that should more accurately have been called "Strategies to Cope with Writing". Now at last the children are really writing — *sustained writing about personally chosen interests* . . . It is achieving excellent results in their handling of writing *and* reading.' — JIM FINDLAY, Resource Teacher, Hurstville South Primary School, who is involved with the approach in four classes, Years 3-4.

CHAPTER 2

Getting Started

This approach to writing is NEW—for the teacher, the parent, the child. Each of these 'human factors' needs to have been *prepared* for the change; so check the 'preparation' ideas on page 16. But no matter how thoroughly you may have prepared, you will surely discover some 'bugs' when you get started. They might originate with . . .

● **Yourself.** Are you finding it hard to relax old do-as-I-tell-you ways? Hard to rely mainly on questioning? Hard to hand over topic-choice and control of the writing to the learner?

● **The Parent.** Have you sufficiently explained the approach to all parents, through meetings and letters? Or are parents saying, 'I can't fathom what the school's up to—it's not the way I was taught to write? Why the sudden change in methods?'

● **The Child.** Have you sufficiently aroused the children's interest in a new approach? . . . 'We are going to learn to write by writing the way real writers write: they choose their own topics, write a draft, get opinions on it, polish for publication' . . . and so on.

● **The Classroom.** Adelaide teachers Jack Mugford and Avril Berndt have devised a chart/checklist to help you get process-conference writing started, whence you can eradicate the 'bugs' as you go [*see next page*].

Avril Berndt and Jack Mugford at work with their Years 4/5 children at Richmond Primary School, Adelaide. They are firm believers in daily writing because 'you learn to write by writing'. They themselves write frequently with the children to provide a model and forge a bond in this 'writing classroom'.

How Writers Improve Their Writing[1]

STEP 1: Find a Topic

Decide what you want to write about.
If you can't immediately do so,
look at your list of topics; or
talk to a friend; or
look at your friend's list; or
talk to your teacher.

STEP 2: Write a Draft

Write your first draft.

STEP 3: Will You Move to Editing?

If you like the draft story, move ahead.
If you don't, go back to Step 1.

STEP 4: Do Your First Editing

Read your story to yourself.
How does it sound? Is anything missing?
Should anything be added to make sense?

STEP 5: Get a Reader's Opinion

Ask at least one friend to read your story.
Listen to your friend's opinions and questions.
Discuss ways to improve the story.

STEP 6: Ask for a Conference

Put your name on the 'Ready for Conference' list.

---

[1] Jack and Avril recommend that the chart be treated as a helpful checklist — but only helpful while getting the class started. (The children refer to it and follow the steps in the writing process.) They stress that it can be taken down after a few weeks because what it says comes to look obvious and far too general, having been overtaken by the children's practical grasp of the approach.

STEP 7: Conference: Questions

Your teacher will ask questions like:
Which part did your friend like best?
Which part do you think needs improving?
Can you suggest some improvements?

STEP 8: Do Your Main Editing

Improve your story in every possible way.
Perhaps, then, write out a second draft.

STEP 9: Ask for Another Conference

Again, put your name on the 'Conference' list.
Be ready to answer all possible questions.

STEP 10: Conference: Everything Considered!

Your teacher will ask questions like:
Is your story now exactly as you want it?
Is it ready for me to read?
Would you please read this part aloud?
Have you checked all punctuation, spelling?
How might you arrange pages, illustrations?

STEP 11: Prepare for Publication

If your story is selected by you and
your teacher for publication, be sure it is
clearly handwritten for our typist-helpers.

STEP 12: Hooray! My Book's to be Published!

Put your manuscript in the typing folder.
(Or arrange to do your own printing.)
Illustrate the book when the typist returns it.

CHAPTER 3

Classroom Organisation

Undoubtedly 'classroom organisation' looms as the main problem for teachers who are about to try the conference approach, especially if they have had little previous experience with individualised or group teaching.

Chapter 3, page 24, provides detailed help in meeting this and other problems. Each of its seven areas deserve application to Years 3-6: (1) Timetabling, (2) Physical Resources, (3) Whether to Use Grouping, (4) How Parent Aides Can Help, (5) Storage and the Writing Folder, (6) What to Do with Published 'Books', (7) How to Make Rules. Moreover, as the children grow older they are better able to work on their own.

Of course, no one will look for perfection straight away. After arousing the children's interest and explaining the changed routines and expectations, Judy Wagner says: 'Look, this is new for all of us. Let's keep discussing the best ways to organise our classroom and we'll make workable rules as we go'. (Oatley West P.S., Year 3 class)

● **Tony Moore on the Conference Approach in Primary Schools of the Liverpool Region (N.S.W.):** 'We realised early that classroom logistics needed rethinking. No longer did we expect completed writing from each lesson. To "give control of the writing to the child" means allowing each child to work at an individual pace and at any length. This led us to appreciate "The Folder" as the mechanism of flexibility; carrying work-in-progress, it permits writing to be put aside, taken up later, or held for a conference . . .

'The scene is always busy. Time is especially at a premium in the early stages when many teachers are reluctant to drop any language lessons in favour of more time for writing; but by the end of the year many had found that "language" could be integrated with the writing period and so save time, without any drop in language performance . . . And "writing" is now seen by some to extend beyond the personal-experience kind to the content areas where, as well as the usual expository forms (notes, reports, etc.), there are lively uses of narrative and poetry.'

● **To Group or Not to Group?** This is probably the chief single point of contention about classroom organisation. The K-2 teachers of the St. George Project were evenly divided about it. There Carolyn Bowman put the no-grouping position clearly: 'I found that grouping wasn't necessary. I think of my Writing Time as a library scene, with everyone working individually or in pairs. They come to me when they need help. Of course I keep a list of names and check it every week.'

On the other hand, Tony Moore found that, 'Generally, I think, the classroom climate and quality of writing were higher in the primary classes that worked in groups. However, grouping is only one factor among many and is difficult to isolate when total class structure varies as often as the number of classes. Every teacher needs to experiment in order to find what is right for him or her.'

CHAPTER 4

The Conference

The nature of the conference and its 'how-to' are explained comprehensively on pages 34-5. A conference is the supreme means of individualising teaching/learning; it is a one-to-one interaction in which the teacher fosters self-learning by the child. Many teachers are grasping the idea that 'conferencing is an art' and are showing pride in practising it.

● **Questioning.** Largely the art is one of questioning, while leaving control of the writing with the child. Jim Findlay is emphatic about this:

> 'In the conference, find yourself a texta colour *that doesn't work.* Then put the lid on it just in case. Don't write on this child's paper! For if you do, you will transfer the responsibility for the writing from the child to the teacher—which is ruinous . . . As to a piece that is really illegible, why not get the child to read it onto tape?'

Questions should be directed, says Julia Smith, at revealing to the child the flexibility latent in the writing process:

> 'For example, Tina's first draft read, "The girl stepped into the mud." I asked her if she could make this interesting for a reader. She started talking about mud and soon found emotive words, her imagination running riot. More questions helped her settle on a few points that she could use in revision to lift the drama of her story.'

Another use of questions is suggested by Trevor Cairney:

> 'If you are hesitant about "picking on weaknesses", why not do this: first, comment on something positive; second, choose to focus on only one or two weaknesses (more will be too many); third, *ask a question about the weakness rather than simply slam it*, e.g. "What do you mean by, 'He was a victim of the law'? I don't follow that." . . . Always ask the writer to explain the meaning that he has not succeeded in conveying.'

And questioning is taken still further by Jack Mugford:

> 'In conference, my first comments highlight strengths in the writing. Questions then probe what the child *knows* about the topic; likewise about the writing conventions, so that I am teaching these in context. Later my focus shifts to form and effectiveness, with questions that invite the child to discover ways to improve skills and content.'

● **Beyond Questioning.** The conference can do more than achieve improvements in the given piece of writing, as Anne Cumming says:

> 'If we see to it that the child experiences success in the conference then *confidence* is boosted and the child wants to write again. Moreover, child-to-child conferences also start to take place—the confidence about solving writing problems is spreading. They talk, listen and read to one another about writing . . . Quantity increases, skills are refined, quality improves . . . The spiral development would leave most educational "kit-makers" green with envy!'

Cathy Hickson sees other ways in which the confidence spreads:

> 'When, through conference, the child feels assured of the teacher's support and realises that the writing can always be polished by editing, then this child becomes a more adventurous writer . . . I see this confidence filtering "across the curriculum", first influencing reading, and then other subjects.'

Jim Findlay has found that the write-publish-read process of the conference approach has boosted the confidence of these children in their ability to read.

Chapter 5

The Writing Time

This chapter deals with the broad stages of the writing process. Most of what was said about these stages in Chapter 5, Part 1, is fully relevant to writing in Years 3-6. But of course there needs to be *growth* — in fluency and in skills, in 'subject' writing and in control of modes of writing (letters, reports, notes, etc.).

1. Topic Choice (see page 43)

Writing at the K-2 level keeps rather naturally a 'personal' or 'experience' focus. This needs to be retained in Years 3-6 whilst widening the focus to cover a good deal of writing in the subject areas:

> 'Must the child's "ownership" of topics and writing end at the threshold of subject writing? Must curriculum prescription and teacher-direction become the order of the day? Definitely not. Primary curriculum provisions are mostly very general. They set only broad limits, and *within those limits there is room for a great deal of topic origination and ownership of writing by the child.* Donald Graves says that when young schoolchildren acquire confidence at making topic-choices in experience-writing they become fit to cope with the content subjects, where some prescription of subject matter is necessary. Even then, one hopes, a teacher will not impose a single topic but will rather allow a degree of choice within a broad frame . . .'[1]

Julia Smith says:

> 'When setting a topic in Natural Science or Social Studies it is a good idea for the teacher to give the children broad headings and then allow them to present information both written and pictorial in their own way. For example, I began a unit on Frogs by asking for 10 minutes 'Quick Writing' of general knowledge. This gave me my start- ing point for programming. I also collated the results as a Data Bank. Then I asked them to find out about (1) appearance, (2) habitat, (3) food, (4) life cycle. Under these broad heads they found they had great individual scope. To finish the unit I asked them (again broadly) to write a related *story* about their backyards—and we achieved great diversity in the flow of ideas of Science to Creative Writing.'

Hilary Mills, a Year 7 Resource Teacher, says:

> 'My children had been so used to writing on teacher-prescribed topics

---

[1] R. D. Walshe, *Every Child Can Write!* (P.E.T.A., 1981), p. 71. This book contains an extensive survey of the whole problem of 'Topics for Writing' in the primary school (pp. 59-120), with detailed attention to the 'subject areas'.

that they found free topic-choice difficult. I decided that more than a topic was involved. So I took them to visit Infants classes. Each child selected an infants 'reader' and discussed his or her interests: this led to choice of a topic for a specific reader. During the writing that followed, the older child would try the piece out on the younger, listen to criticism, then polish it. The interchange worked well.' (Hurstville Boys' High School)

Judy Wagner tells how she handles new modes of writing:

'If I want my class to learn how to write, say, a play, I go first to good models. We gather a number from the library, then read, act and discuss parts of them. At the right moment I suggest that individuals or groups might try to turn one of their previously "published" stories into a play . . .' (Oatley West P.S.)

2. Drawing (see page 47)

The function of drawing as a pre-writing organiser of thought is at its height in the K-1 years. From that time the children seem increasingly to 'internalise' their pictures by visualising them in the mind without needing to draw them. But this change varies in time and completeness from one child to the next. So why not leave to primary children the option of associating drawing with writing?

Some children, indeed, continue well into secondary school to value drawing as an adjunct to writing. Moreover there is a related pressure from subject areas such as Science, Social Studies and Health to link sketches, diagrams, maps and flowcharts with writing. Julia Smilth finds interesting her observation that Years 3-4 children, undirected as to presentation of a Science topic, will divide between those who illustrate first then write and those who do the reverse.

3. Draft Writing (using 'invented spelling') (see page 51)

The key principle of the conference approach—that 'ownership' of the writing must be kept in the young writer's hands—requires not only freedom of topic-choice but also *freedom in the writing of the first draft* (and later in editing it). So nothing should be done that deflects the child's attention from getting meaning (content) onto paper, for clarifying and correcting can come later, at the editing stage.

But newcomers to the approach will not naturally use their freedom-to-draft to good purpose. Jim Findlay found that many primary children were at first 'tied to the single-page syndrome' or, worse, the 'three-sentence syndrome'—they finish off abruptly when they have written little more than an introduction! ('Yet it is hard,' he laments, 'to argue with the conclusiveness of some snap endings: "And then I woke up!" or "At that point a Russian bomb blew up the world!" ') *So the teacher must emphasise that there is unlimited time and space to write a story.*

However, he realises from working with slow learners that not all children should be made to write every day, 'especially early in the program'. They should nevertheless be asked to *do something connected with writing*: illustrate published books, read peers' books, research, etc. 'I'm content if these children write on three days out of five. At least when they then write they have something constructive to write about.'

Some primary teachers unhesitatingly continue the principles of 'invented spelling' in Years 3-6, dispensing entirely with separate spelling lessons and lists. Jack Mugford, for instance, won't provide a spelling until the child has *attempted* to work it out on paper. He continually encourages the writing down of words they need but can't spell, reminding them that first-draft spellings can be checked later. Other teachers while pursuing a similar course also allow the child time each week to compile an *individual word list* drawn from (1) the week's personal writing, (2) words used currently in subject areas, (3) word frequency lists, which are made available, (4) words considered topical by the teacher.

4. Preparing for Publication (see page 58)

The point made for the K-2 years continues to be true for the 3-6 years: *don't deal with editing as a set of exercises but rather as a necessary act of polishing those special pieces of writing that will be published.*

In the primary school the teachers strive to create the spirit of a 'writing community' in which everyone helps everyone else. As well as the teacher helping the child in conference, several expedients are possible: (1) children work in pairs as 'writing partners'; (2) small groups share writing in order to obtain suggestions; (3) every day several pieces are read to the whole class and discussed; (4) children from a more senior primary class or a secondary school visit to make suggestions (similarly, the visited class visits a more junior class to help them — which probably does even more for the helpers than the helped!).

All in the Mind

'Stephanie, how do you decide what you'll write next?'
  'I draw pictures . . . then I write about the best.'
  'But I haven't seen you drawing before you write.'
  'Oh, I draw in my mind,' said the shy 6 year old.
  'When do you do that?'
  'M-m-m, in the bath, coming to school, just anywhere.'
  'Will you ever run out of pictures to write about?'
  'No, I keep thinking of more and more when I write and read.'

CHAPTER 6

Publishing the Writing

Look at page 61 for ways to go about publishing. The main point is: 'The essence of "publication" is not just producing a "book"; it is getting writing to real readers—*getting it read*.' Here are some of the gains that accrue to a 'publish-and-read' writing classroom:

.. Publication stimulates writing—writers like to be published;
.. it impels the writer to study the projected readership;
.. it cultivates 'real writing', i.e. writing meant to be read;
.. it influences the writer to strive for excellence;
.. it prompts study of various writing modes, for various purposes;
.. it improves reading because the writing is read with interest;
.. it exerts peer pressure on reluctant readers to do *some* reading;
.. it enables the class to produce many of its own texts and materials, all written at an appropriate level;
.. similarly, it enables the class to produce learning materials for more junior classes, in the knowledge that the juniors look up to the older children and readily receive their 'message'.

'You Will See a Marked Improvement in Attitude . . .'

As a Resource Teacher, Jim Findlay has found that the write-publish-read process of the conference approach works wonders with reluctant learners. He instances Jillian in Year 3:

> 'At the beginning of the program Jillian said, "I can't read! I know I can't read!" But after a month, when she had had two stories published, she said of one of them, "Of course I can read it. I wrote it." Later she said, "I want to write a play. Do you have a magazine with a play in it?" She had developed enough confidence to try a new mode *and to read* in order to find an appropriate model.'

Handling Publication

The physical problems of publishing in primary classes are not very different from those discussed for K-2 (pages 62-3), but there may be less reliance on typing by parent aides and more production by the children themselves.

Most teachers will be inclined to see 'publication' as something limited to the classroom, the readers being the children and the teacher. Others will want to go further and at least reach parents and other classes.[1] But Cobden Primary School[2] in a rural area of Victoria has shown that 'three

---

[1] See the detailed analysis of potential readers for a schoolchild's writing in R. D. Walshe's *Every Child Can Write!* (P.E.T.A., 1981), p. 51.
[2] 'We would love to share our books and our experience with anyone wishing to do the same sort of thing,' write Barbara Kerr, Bruce Mitchell and Rosalie Moorfield, Cobden P.S., Victoria St., Cobden, Vic. 3266.

Authors working on one of the books published imaginatively by Cobden Primary School and distributed widely throughout rural Victoria. The project began with a resolve to 'throw away some of those awful readers' cluttering the storeroom shelves and replace them with interesting books written by the children.

or four interested teachers and parents' can launch a much more exciting publishing venture . . . It began with the resolve to 'throw away some of those awful readers sitting unread on the storeroom shelves'—and to replace them with books written by the children.

Five things, the Cobdenites decided, were needed in setting up a school publishing company. *First*, a helpful printer—they found one, an ex-teacher, with an offset press. *Second*, a distribution network—they contacted all newsagents, booksellers and schools for 100 km around (and sold out a 900 print run in two weeks!). *Third*, illustrators—they found able volunteers easily. *Fourth*, authors—there were 'about 75 of them, bursting to be included', eager for conferences, willing to follow an arduous write-discuss-edit-rewrite program. *Fifth*, funds—they raised a capital of $700.00. They have made a 'slight profit' on the venture and are now planning more books . . . 'Not only have we provided more suitable texts, but the biggest gain has been in making the children enthusiastic writers.'

CHAPTER 7

Programming and Evaluation

1. Simplified Programming (see page 64)

For Years 3-6 as for K-2, the program of the conference approach can be expressed either in a single sentence or the half-page outline offered by Robyn Platt. In a word, the approach *is* the program. For the rest, as Jim Findlay says bluntly, 'Establish your routines for daily writing and stick to them.'

For the primary years, Cathy Hickson adds her observation that, 'The trend of the approach is towards *language integration*: the children write/read and out of this comes a flow of "language" which would previously have been chopped up under such heads as handwriting, spelling, vocabulary, usage, grammar, comprehension, reading, writing, and thinking skills. But now there is neither time nor reason for all these artificial categories. The children *write* and this is simultaneously a time of reading, spelling, vocabulary and all the rest!'

2. Evaluation (see page 66)

The universal testimony of teachers who have tried the conference approach is: 'Because of frequent conferences and frequent reading of what the children have written about their self-chosen interests, we know every child much more deeply than ever before.'

To supplement this understanding, however, most primary teachers seem to make use of (1) some kind of *record book* in which an anecdotal 'profile' is built up, chiefly by jottings after conferences; (2) some kind of periodic *sampling*, such as three pieces per term of each child's best writing.

The Years 3-6 teachers are just as concerned as the K-2 teachers to keep the parents fully informed of the new approach and of their children's progress. They realise that this cannot be done honestly by giving a numerical mark nor by stock phrases such as 'Not working to capacity' or 'Could show more care'. Delighted by the children's heightened interest in writing, the teachers are pleased to tell the parents about real and specific progress.

• **Avril Berndt and Jack Mugford.** 'The children now enjoy writing, want to write, often write at home . . . Quality has clearly improved . . . They work cooperatively, helping one another . . . An upsurge of interest in words . . . Quantity has increased without detracting from quality . . . There are positive effects for reading.'

• **Jim Findlay.** 'An enormous boost to confidence . . . They are trying out new styles without teacher direction . . . Both quantity and quality have improved . . . There is use of more precise language.'

• **Julia Smith.** 'The effects on E.S.L. children are splendid . . . Metin (Turkish, with little English at home, and poor communication skills) has made outstanding progress, is now sequencing ideas well, has acquired a sense of structure, his imagination seems to have been released . . .'

CHAPTER 8

'Not Only Writing Improves . . .'

Teachers of Years 3-6, like those of K-2 (see page 70), have reported many beneficial by-products of this approach to writing. Let me summarise these and offer a tentative explanation.

1. *Component Elements of Writing Improve*. As well as the writing itself (clarity, style), many components are seen to improve:

> *handwriting*, because it is so often read by others;
>
> *spelling*, because it loses its fears, through 'invented spelling';
>
> *punctuation*, because it is seen as an aid for readers;
>
> *word-interest*, because there is constant attention to effectiveness;
>
> *sentence-flexibility*, because 'Now I know I can say it in many ways'.

2. *Reading Improves*. This is the nearly universal observation of teachers, and it usually comes after only a couple of months of operation of the conference approach to writing. Some also say that range of reading-interests widens.

3. *Learners Grow More Confident*. The third most common observation is that children's confidence extends beyond writing and reading to learning in general.

4. *Behaviour Improves*. Perhaps this observation is to be expected, as a corollary of the children's heightened confidence as learners.

5. *Learning 'Across-the-Curriculum' Improves*. This happens not only because of the general increase in learning-confidence but because writing in particular has an important place in the many 'content areas' of the curriculum.

6. *Learning by E.S.L. Children Improves*. The child for whom English is a second language seems to respond warmly to all the main principles of the approach: individual conference, free topic-choice, 'invented spelling', 'ownership' of the writing, the process of drafting-editing-publishing, and ample time to write.

7. *Learning by 'Remedial' Children Improves*. The approach is quickly winning friends among teachers concerned with so-called 'slow', 'reluctant', 'troublesome', and 'remedial' learners—especially (so far) for its successes with writing, reading and spelling. (See 'A Remedial-Reading-through-Writing Program', by Jan Turbill, in *Every Child Can Write!*, by R. D. Walshe, P.E.T.A., 1981.)

How to Explain These Many Improvements?

A powerful case can be made for the importance—even *centrality*—of writing in school learning. An era is ending in which writing was mostly treated as handwriting plus rather mechanical 'composition'. Now writing is increasingly seen as thinking itself. It is a specially careful kind of thinking: *thinking made visible on the page*, where the ideas can be subjected to a process of revision and so clarified.

Writing conceived in this way demands from the writer substantial information, economy of thought, logical sequencing of ideas, concern for the reader, and concern for style. It is this *improvement in thinking/learning power* that is being achieved by the conference approach with effects that not surprisingly are extending beyond writing to the whole curriculum.

'Just think—the literate masses!'

'Yes, I'm converted! . . . The basis of the approach is the confidence it inspires. Every child, feeling confident in this environment, writes willingly; then, receiving attention and praise, writes again. A cycle! The confident readiness to write guarantees quantity, but skills are watched by the other children as well as by the teacher and so the quality grows . . . I'm enthusiastic when I see my class's results, achieved in so short a time. Next year, knowing what I now know, things will be even better . . . The mind soars! Just think—the literate masses!'

Anne Cumming, Newbridge Heights P.S.

Teachers and Schools of the St. George Writing Project K-2

● **Grays Point Public School** (Grays Point, N.S.W. 2232)
Robyn Platt (Mistress): Year 2: 15 girls, 9 boys
Debbie Brownjohn: Year 1: 16 girls, 14 boys
Wendy Goebel: Year 2: 13 girls, 13 boys
Lurline Grime: Kindergarten: 11 girls, 12 boys
Judy Harris: Year 1: 18 girls, 13 boys
Linda Mein: Kindergarten: 14 girls, 8 boys

● **Hurstville South Public School** (Hurstville South, N.S.W. 2221)
Robyn Legge (Mistress): Year 1: 15 girls, 19 boys
Janeen Bartlett: Year 1: 14 girls, 13 boys
Carolyn Bowman: Year 2: 12 girls, 15 boys
Jim Findlay: Resource: Years 1-6
Margaret Newton: Kindergarten: 13 girls, 12 boys
Pat Robertson: Kindergarten: 15 girls, 12 boys
Chris Small: E.S.L.: Years 1-6
Robyn Smith: Year 2: 14 girls, 14 boys
Ruth Staples: Year 2: 16 girls, 11 boys

● **Sylvania Heights Public School** (Sylvania, N.S.W. 2224)
Barbara Fiala (Mistress)
Judy Antoniolli: Year 2: 17 girls, 14 boys
Evelyn Collaro: Year 2: 16 girls, 14 boys
Margaret Cooper: Year 1: 16 girls, 12 boys
Therese Corben: Year 2: 13 girls, 11 boys
Joan Ham: Kindergarten: 17 girls, 14 boys
Christa Hunt: Year 1: 15 girls, 14 boys
Liz Marshall: Comp. 1/2: 5 girls, 18 boys
Fiona Powning: Kindergarten: 13 girls, 14 boys
Marilyn Rigg: Year 1: 19 girls, 10 boys
Joan Smollett: Year 2: 17 girls, 13 boys
Karen Wade: Comp. 1/2: 11 girls, 11 boys
Sue Wyndham: Kindergarten: 14 girls, 14 boys

Index